MW00574008

THE SAMURAI SWORD

THE
SAMURAI
SWORD

SPIRIT • STRATEGY • TECHNIQUES

Kohshyu Yoshida

TUTTLE Publishing

Tokyo | Rutland, Vermont | Singapore

This book is dedicated to The Truth, Light and Righteousness.

Please note that the publisher and author of this instructional book are NOT RESPONSIBLE in any manner whatsoever for any injury that may result from practicing the techniques and/or following the instructions given within. Martial arts training can be dangerous—both to you and to others—if not practiced safely. If you're in doubt as to how to proceed or whether your practice is safe, consult with a trained martial arts teacher before beginning. Since the physical activities described herein may be too strenuous in nature for some readers, it is also essential that a physician be consulted prior to training.

Published by Tuttle Publishing, an imprint of Periplus Editions (HK) Ltd., with editorial offices at 364 Innovation Drive, North Clarendon, Vermont 05759 U.S.A.

Copyright © 2009 Kohshyu Yoshida. All rights reserved. No part of this publication may be reproduced or utilized in any form or by any means, electronic or mechanical, including photocopying, recording, or by any information storage and retrieval system, without prior written permission from the publisher.

Library of Congress Cataloging-in-Publication Data

Yoshida, Kohshyu.
 The Samurai sword : spirit, strategy, techniques / Kohshyu Yoshida.
   p. cm.
 ISBN 978-0-8048-3751-4 (pbk.)
 1. Swordplay—Japan. 2. Martial arts—Japan. 3. Samurai.
   I. Title.
 GV1150.Y67 2009
 796.860952--dc22   2009019411

Credits
Editor: Scot Lewis. Photographer and Art Designer: Kenji Hashimoto. Photography studio: Southern California Taekwondo Center. DVD video recording by Ryo Fujimura.

How to Download the Demonstration Videos

1. You must have an Internet connection.
2. Type the URL below into to your web browser.

https://www.tuttlepublishing.com/the-samurai-sword-video

For support, email us at
info@tuttlepublishing.com

Distributed by
North America, Latin America & Europe
Tuttle Publishing
364 Innovation Drive
North Clarendon, VT 05759-9436 U.S.A.
Tel: 1 (802) 773-8930; Fax: 1 (802) 773-6993
info@tuttlepublishing.com
www.tuttlepublishing.com

Japan
Tuttle Publishing
Yaekari Building 3rd Floor
5-4-12 Osaki
Shinagawa-ku
Tokyo 141-0032
Tel: (81) 3 5437-0171; Fax: (81) 3 5437-0755
sales@tuttle.co.jp
www.tuttle.co.jp

Asia Pacific
Berkeley Books Pte. Ltd.
3 Kallang Sector #04-01,
Singapore 349278
Tel: (65) 6741 2178; Fax: (65) 6741 2179
inquiries@periplus.com.sg
www.tuttlepublishing.com

First edition
22 21 20 19   7 6 5 4 3

Printed in Hong Kong   1907EP

TUTTLE PUBLISHING® is a registered trademark of Tuttle Publishing, a division of Periplus Editions (HK) Ltd.

ABOUT TUTTLE: "Books to Span the East and West"

Our core mission at Tuttle Publishing is to create books which bring people together one page at a time. Tuttle was founded in 1832 in the small New England town of Rutland, Vermont (USA). Our fundamental values remain as strong today as they were then—to publish best-in-class books informing the English-speaking world about the countries and peoples of Asia. The world has become a smaller place today and Asia's economic, cultural and political influence has expanded, yet the need for meaningful dialogue and information about this diverse region has never been greater. Since 1948, Tuttle has been a leader in publishing books on the cultures, arts, cuisines, languages and literatures of Asia. Our authors and photographers have won numerous awards and Tuttle has published thousands of books on subjects ranging from martial arts to paper crafts. We welcome you to explore the wealth of information available on Asia at **www.tuttlepublishing.com**.

ACKNOWLEDGMENTS

I would like to express my gratitude to those people who have always believed in me and supported me so faithfully in many ways. Scot Lewis, you are a great editor, my Taekwondo teacher, and more than anything, you are a man with a true good heart. You really know what patience is. Pam Lewis, our personal trainer and Scot's wife, thank you for your strong support of Scot and myself.

Kenji Hashimoto, I could not have survived and completed most of my works without your help. You are truly a great artist and true friend with pure loyalty.

Ohno Sasaki & Daniel Tam-Lung. You are both true mentors and teachers of art and life. You are two highly spiritual people. Ohno Sasaki is a direct descendant of legendary samurai 佐々木盛綱 Moritsuna Sasaki, and I feel very honored to know you as I am also a descendant of a samurai. I am constantly learning about how humans should live from both of you. Thank you so much for being in my life. I am truly honored.

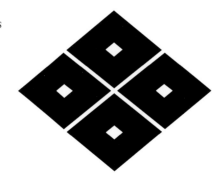

Thank you very much and I wish you much happiness.

KOHSHYU YOSHIDA

日のヤマト

CONTENTS

LIVE YOUR
TRUTH

*A man possesses extraordinary skills
and lives to serve his heart.*

The concept behind the phrase **Live Your Truth** is very strongly rooted in samurai and Zen principles. Zen teaching often encourages living faithfully to your heart. Stay true to yourself otherwise you are not truly living with integrity. Adhering to this simple but strong teaching in your life will bring calmness and peacefulness to your heart. It will make your life complete. The samurai learned to constantly look into his heart. This principle really connected the samurai's mind and heart. As warriors who could face danger at any time in their life, they learned to take joy in the beautiful moments of daily life. They didn't want to feel regret in their hearts for letting these moments pass by unheeded. So, this aspect of Zen teaching was strongly emphasized. The author still follows this principle because life is not really about how long we live, it's more about *how* we live.

In today's world, we tend to live longer, but it doesn't necessarily mean that we have more contentment in our hearts; on the contrary, the opposite is often true. Ultimately, human value is not always about actions and possessions, it's more about our pure existence. We just need to realize this to make ourselves stronger.

"A man possesses extraordinary skills and lives to serve his heart."

This saying reminds us that samurai were all men with extraordinary skill as warriors, yet they were dedicated to trying to live with a clear mind and pure heart. It should be our goal to do likewise.

心力いずれば事を成し、事なさるれば和に至る。

When the strength in your heart flows out, things will become complete and the completion will bring harmony.

Koh Ryu Do: The Light in Our Heart

We can grow our light into a star. And a star will burst forward into multiple points of light. And each one of those points of light is like a sword, and it can diminish all negativity and bring cleansing to this world.

Koh Ryu Do is my original term for my life philosophy, which applies to all the various aspects of our lives. 光 **Koh** indicates light. 流 **Ryu** means flow. And 道 **Do** designates the avenue through your heart. Though it may have the familiar ring of a particular brand of martial art, the term doesn't necessarily refer to a specific style. It carries various meanings and should be applied to the wider scope of one's life.

In general, the expression 道 **Do**, or 'way,' has always been used as the indication of a style, method, or system as well as a journey or path. But I emphasize Do as an avenue within your heart in addition to the traditional meaning commonly used in reference to martial arts styles.

Why did I come up with this idea? The germ for the idea came to me when I realized that, ultimately, physical techniques are not the most important aspects of life. Whatever stage of life you find yourself in, now is the time for self-realization and to bring internal peace to your heart. Of course, the physical aspect is also important but it is of relatively minimal concern when we come to realize that we are ultimately more spiritual beings than physical beings. We reach a point after many years of training where the level of our physical ability limits our power and techniques. But the human heart (spirit) is the original power source that has no limitation. This means the power of the heart is infinite because it's connected directly to the universe.

天照大御神 **Amaterasu Oomikami** is the protective Goddess over Japan, as well as the 太陽神 **God of the Sun**. Koh Ryu Do indicates 太陽光 sun and light with the character 光 **Koh** to protect us on our journey. But to know Amaterasu Oomikami better, we need to know Shinto.

神道 **Shinto**, the Way of God, is the universal (cosmic) philosophy and spiritual teachings that was born in Japan during ancient times. Shinto teaches about the origin of human existence, which is the heart itself, and our heart is the pure existence of a luminous being. Though our existence is a combination of the physical and spiritual, the spiritual portion of the equation is of greater value, as the spirit doesn't die after our physical death.

I created the term Koh Ryu Do to share this universal concept with the rest of the world. Our existence is full of positive and negative experiences. Though the negatives bring us down at times, Koh Ryu Do, the Light in Our Heart, will always help to bring us back up.

Light flows out of your heart.

CHAPTER 1

THE WAY OF
THE SAMURAI

*The samurai of armor on the
left Toyoharakitajima Shrine
豊原北嶋神社. It is a national
treasure which originally belonged
to Moritsuna Sasaki 佐々木盛綱.
He was the warlord of Genji 源氏
in twelfth century Japan.*

S amurai were soldiers hired to protect their lord, their land and its people. In the beginning, they were simply soldiers, but as time passed and family heritages were built, the samurai became stronger warriors with the philosophy of the universe in their minds and hearts. They respected their enemies as much as they respected themselves, so when a samurai warrior killed an enemy, he did so very honorably. That way he would receive an honorable death, too. The battle was sacred to them.

In the Chinese character alphabet the word 侍 **samurai** is a combination of 人 **Person** and 寺 **Temple**. Zen, or meditation, which is famous in the world today, was helpful to the samurai in ancient times to maintain inner peace.

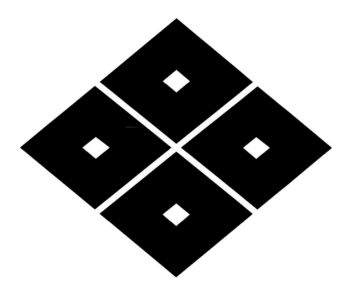

While some samurai were purely militaristic, others were spiritual warriors who tried to understand the world and its contradictions. These warriors were honored to protect people rather than kill them. Their sword was a spiritual symbol of commitment, a legacy, and a receptacle for their soul. Their practice of calligraphy and poetry were their way of sharing their internal space with others.

There is a legend that a true samurai will be reborn to protect his country when it faces danger. In the nineteenth century, Shyoin Yoshida said, "Even though your body dies, the samurai spirit will live forever." Today, the Japanese people still look to the samurai warrior and his philosophy for inspiration.

The family crest of Moritsuna Sasaki, who was the warlord of Genji 源氏 *in the twelfth century.*

The cherry blossom is another samurai symbol. This is because the cherry tree blooms for a very short time and then the flowers are gone. Like the samurai warrior, the cherry blossom dies at the peak of its maturity. Today, the cherry blossom is the national flower of Japan. I sometimes think about the cherry blossom and send my blessings in honor of them, as I am one of them.

The term 士道 **Shido** means "The Way of the Samurai." The ultimate warriors' code of honor, the Way of the Samurai is to "protect your truth." Never betray yourself. A samurai would choose death over living with an untrue heart.

The samurai have existed for about 1,100 years in Japan. Before they established their samurai code they were called *tsuwamono* or *mononofu* then finally samurai.

Also, the Japanese royal family 天皇家 **Ten Nou Ke** has existed for around 3,000 years. By some accounts it has existed since before the dawn of recorded history.

The word samurai literally means to "serve." So they protected the royal family and eventually other lords. The samurai belief system can be explained by the ancient Japanese faith called 神道 **Shinto** or "the Way of God." Shinto represents ancient Japanese history, and culture and parallels many Native American beliefs. Native Americans and Japanese carry the same DNA because they are both part of the same ancient Japanese family. This is because humans migrated from Japan and Mongolia to other lands such as Alaska, North America and South America. Another similarity between the Japanese and Native Americans is the totem pole. The Japanese have an ancient custom of praying to God through a tree pole similar to the Native American totem pole.

The Ten Nou Ke Japanese royal family crest is a chrysanthemum blossom.

Later, as Buddhism and Zen philosophy came to Japan, the samurai combined and blended Zen teachings with Shinto in an interesting way. They constantly practiced Zen to understand life. Zen practice became very natural to them because their lifestyle was already very meditative.

士風 Shi Fuu: Samurai Manners

The straight translation of Shi Fuu is "the Wind of the Samurai." The earth produces wind to express its life. Likewise, Shi Fuu blows from the samurai's heart so that others can sense it. One who lives with a samurai's heart will show it more than talk about it. It shows in their presence. It's the same as the contrast between someone merely talking about the teachings of the Bible and one actually *living* the teachings. It's always easier to "talk the talk" than to actually "walk the walk." But if Shi Fuu is true to your heart, it should not be so difficult to express. Others can then appreciate one's "wind."

There are three essences that can show up in your "wind." They are *wisdom*, *love* and *courage*. If they are adequately present within your heart, they will make you a good leader as well.

- **On Wisdom:** Sharpen your wisdom, so that you can see what you need to do in the bigger picture.

- **On Love:** Connect with the universe, so that you will understand others as your fellows.

- **On Courage:** Understand life, so that fear will be a friend of your heart. You will be able to accomplish life's missions without having fear attached to it. The universe will accept the true warrior who faces his fears and overcomes obstacles by expanding the range of mind power, heart and spirit. Your body will follow your soul.

福沢諭吉 **Yukichi Fukuzawa**, a 19th century samurai, was the founder of Keio University in Tokyo. He was also one of the first representatives of Japan to come to the United States. Fukuzawa left behind a very strong message that "We need to emphasize, teach and pass Shi Fuu to future generations."

士風 **Shi Fuu**—*The Wind of the Samurai*

CHAPTER 2

THE SPIRIT
OF THE
SAMURAI

Samurai virtues are the contents of our heart,
and these contents are "Light."

Battle is Sacred

The samurai believed that you respect your enemy because he is reflecting a version of yourself. In the beginning of samurai history, during the Genpei period, one-on-one battle was based on the warrior's honor. The combatants made sure to respect and recognize each other. They also had very strong self-respect based on the warrior's ethical teachings of 士道 **Shido**. For example, a samurai would never attempt a sneak attack from behind as this would be disrespectful. According to the samurai code, you will either win or lose with beauty and dignity. Also, samurai believed that their karma and their opponent's karma brought them together. Since it was their fate to battle this opponent, it was the samurai's duty to accept and take responsibility for the outcome.

Some of these rules changed over time with engagements with foreign armies. One of the first changes occurred during the invasion of the Mongolian army in southern Japan during the 13th century. This was due to the fact that the Mongolian army greatly outnumbered the Japanese as well as possessing more advanced weapons such as cannon, poisoned arrows, and sophisticated archery capable of continuous shooting during engagement. It was actually a miracle that the samurai were able to defeat the Mongolian army. Also, the Mongolians didn't respect the warrior's ethic as the samurai did. It was difficult for the samurai to accept this different way of fighting. Where the samurai were used to actually knowing whom they were fighting personally, they now had to fight against an unknown enemy in a group. The etiquette previously displayed in battle was virtually abandoned.

The experience fighting the Mongolians taught the samurai that some warriors have no ethics in battle. This caused the samurai to hold onto their Shido even stronger. Though war is not pretty, there can still be a human and ethical aspect to it.

Fighting is a vice.

This still applies in today's world. If one does whatever one wants to get where and what one wants, the world would be in chaos. It's very easy for us to fight on many levels. There are many situations that frustrate, upset, and tempt us. And fighting, whether physically or verbally, at first seems to fulfill and stimulate your heart as you get caught up in the moment with your opposition. But though fighting may be the easy choice, it doesn't mean that it's the correct choice. We should strive to maintain our humanity and civility no matter the situation. Even if disaster strikes, there should still be an ethical bottom line in those situations.

Our battle should not be fighting for its own sake, but rather we should fight not to have to fight. That is Warriorism (Heroism). It's all up to us.

We must respect "compassion" as Light's central virtue. Compassion is love and nothing can go beyond love. This is the highest virtue to which we can aspire. As a good leader, one has to have strong compassion. If you possess a very clever mind but lack compassion, then, you will always come up short.

Please don't forget, "The heart is wiser than the mind."

Historically, samurai heroes followed the Light within them. Their lives can teach us how we can lead better lives that are free of strife. The Way of the Samurai (the Way of the Martial Arts) is the way of humanity and the way of God.

Ancient Heroes 戦国英雄

Shingen Harunobu Takeda
武田信玄-晴信 1521–1573

Honorific name: 壮 **Magnificent**
Sword name: 真利 **Mari**

Shingen and Kenshin Uesugi were very famous in Japan for the major battles between them that lasted for twelve years. Both Shingen and Kenshin earned great admiration by acting with true samurai spirit and following the warrior's code. Though they were rivals they had the utmost respect for one another. Shingen's philosophy in battle was called 風林火山 **Fuu Rin Ka Zan**. "Fuu" means wind. "Rin" means forest. "Ka" means

Though famous in life, the details of Shingen's demise are not certain. He is buried in what is now Kōshū, Yamanashi Prefecture in Japan.

fire. And "zan" means mountain. Though his troops were the strongest force on the battlefield, his remarkable decision was not to bring a gun into battle even though Westerners had already brought the gun to Japan and some other warlords were using them. Shingen insisted that the concept of the gun would wipe Shido from Japan's landscape. In other words, people will start do anything as long as they can win. That is the way of the beast, not the way of the warrior.

His beliefs and words:

> *"If you win over a hundred battles, it is not virtue.*
>
> *If you win without the battle, it is true virtue."*
>
> *"People are like a castle and gate. Compassion is an asset and hate is the enemy."*

It doesn't matter how strongly you build your castle if you lose people's hearts. Compassion will unite people and cause the country to prosper, but hate will destroy the country. This is why Shingen lived in a castle surrounded by a very simple gate rather than a tall firm gate.

> *"If your triumph is 50%, that is excellent. If your triumph is 70%, that is good.*
>
> *If your triumph is 100%, that is fair."*

A fifty-percent result will make you think about putting in more effort. A seventy-percent result will make you lazy. And a one hundred-percent result will make you over-confident. This principle can be applied to all aspects of life.

The crest of Shingen Takeda.

Kenshin Kagetora Uesugi
上杉謙信-景虎 1530–1578

Honorific name: 心 **Heart**
Sword name: 姫鶴一文字 **Hime Zuru Ichimonji**

He always sensed that he was a reincarnation of Bishya-Monten.

Due to his passion for the Zen philosophy of peace, Kenshin Uesugi didn't often fight for political reasons. On many occasions his political associates asked him to go to war with them. But he was so well respected that he was able to convince his allies that battle was not always the proper avenue to achieve their goals. Kenshin Uesugi respected the value of Zen teachings that claim "if things are not true to your heart, you should not follow and act on them." This was especially true with respect to war. If he didn't see justice in a battle, he didn't engage. Kenshin was a true spiritual warrior.

The crest of Kenshin Uesugi.

The Battle of Kawanakajima really reflected remarkable Shi Fuu. They treated their battle as being very sacred. After fighting for many years, Shingen's army faced the problem of dwindling food and water supply. But rather than take advantage of

his adversary's weakness, Kenshin sent salt to Shingen's side to save their lives. That way Shingen's army could continue to fight to the best of their ability. Though it sounds contrary to most philosophies of battle, Kenshin showed respect and compassion for his opponent. That is how Shido works. Kenshin's thoughts were very pure and very noble.

Kenshin's death poem refers to his feeling that his 49 years had passed like one night's dream.

His beliefs and words:

"If we do not have flaws in our hearts, we need not be afraid of people."

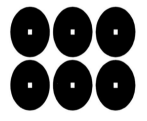

The crest of Yukimura Sanada.

Sanada Yukimura's armor, in the collection of the Osaka Museum.

Yukimura Nobushige Sanada
真田幸村-信繁 1567–1615

Honorific name: 智 **Wisdom**
Sword name: 村正 **Muramasa**

His tactics were like magic. He controlled his people as easily as he controlled his arms and legs. Though they may have wanted to retreat, he convinced them to charge forward. He was also said to be able to communicate his desires to his followers silently. He was a genius warlord. He didn't have as many troops at his disposal as other armies, but he could still hold his own against his larger foes.

At different times, Sanada was referred to as "a hero who may appear once in a hundred years" and "the crimson demon of war."

His beliefs and words:

"If you just focus on personal desire and gain,
and not on respecting the value of grace and duty,
how can we think of you as a human being."

19th Century Heroes 幕末英雄

Ryoma was a visionary who saw modernization as the path to Japan's survival.

Ryoma Naonari Sakamoto
坂本龍馬-直柔 1835–1867

Honorific name: 傑 Hero
Sword name: 陸奥守吉行 Mutsunokami Yoshiyuki

Today Ryoma Sakamoto is known as the "Miracle of the Meiji Restoration." He was a revolutionary who became a pioneer in many fields. From the time he was a child he always questioned and challenged how society and the world worked around him. And this marvelous personality managed to save his country by supporting the restoration of the Meiji emperor through an alliance with his worst of enemies. He had the spirit of a samurai and the talent of a businessman and negotiator.

Ryoma Sakamoto persevered with the concept of the "Sword of the Mind" to find his way. This is the samurai spirit: to fight through the impossible and make it possible.

His beliefs and words:

"We are born to fill a mission in this world. So when death approaches us, we should not be afraid of it. We can accept that it is a time of spiritual promotion."

"I do not take time to get depressed, I would rather think about my next movement."

"A hero is a man who lives on his own path."

"If you are a man with ambition, then you better die falling forward."

The crest of Ryoma Sakamoto.

Falling forward rather than backward means you never stop attempting to achieve your goals.

Shintarou Nakaoka
中岡慎太郎 1838–1867

He was a sidekick of Ryoma. They developed a strong bond to save Japan during the Meiji Restoration. They were both from the Tosa clan.

His beliefs and words:

"The word 'Battle' occupies my mind for the sake of taking the government down."

"Being humble (humility) is about being honorable and not being over confident."

Shintarou Nakaoka was assassinated in Kyoto in 1867 along with Ryoma Sakamoto.

Takamori Takanaga Saigou
西郷隆盛-隆永 1828–1877

Honorific name: 忠 Loyalty
Sword name: 山城信国 Yama Shiro Nobukuni

He is the original **Last Samurai** 最後の侍 from the 19th century. This came about because he was there from the beginning of the Meiji Restoration period and his death coincided with the end of the samurai period. He became a great leader of the Satsuma clan of which Kagoshima was prefect.

Takamori, who disagreed with the potential battle between the samurai and progressive diplomats, asked to be appointed ambassador to Korea. Korea was not happy with Japan's possible alliances with Westerners, so there was animosity that Takamori wanted to try to quell. Rather than allowing Takamori to find a peaceful and honorable solution to mend the relationship with Korea, the Meiji government

The crest of Takamori Saigou.

Saigou led the Satsuma Rebellion, and met his end in battle against Meiji forces in 1877.

had a plan called Sei Kan Ron that employed the armed forces to deal with the situation. This led Takamori to leave the government altogether and become the leader of a new samurai resistance movement against the Meiji government.

Takamori's resistance ended with his death at the Battle of Sei Nan. This was the battle depicted in the film *The Last Samurai*. Some present-day scholars actually believe that Takamori may have been able to win the battle with the help of the other samurai armies. And they think Takamori may have chosen to die for country's sake so that the new Meiji government could lead the nation into a modern era without the in-fighting with the samurai. Takamori wished that the new Japan would be born as quickly as possible so that it would not have to suffer and become a colony of Westerners. Philosophically speaking, the samurai way died with Takamori because with his sacrifice, all other samurai could not continue the fight without dishonoring his wish.

Takamori's name means "prosperity." He died wishing prosperity for the new Japan. He studied hard and connected with the wisdom of the universe, so he was able to handle great changes and destruction in chaotic times. He was the man who had true loyalty and a pure heart. That is why he is called *The Last Samurai*.

His beliefs and words:

"A man should not be distracted by what others say; we should listen to what the dictates for us. We need to try our best for Heaven. And we should continue to ask ourselves how strong our sincerity is."

"A person with stupidity will only focus on self-gain. A person with wisdom can think about gain for all. Self-gain is 'I,' gain is for everyone. A public mind will be blessed, while a 'me' mentality will fail."

敬天愛人 *"Respect Heaven and love the people."*

Kaishyu Yoshikuni Katsu

勝海舟-義邦 1823-1899

Kaishyu Katsu was a naval officer, diplomat and educator.

Honorific name: 師 Mentor
Sword name: 肥前忠吉 Hizen Tada Yoshi

Like Shyoin Yoshida, Kaishyu Katsu had advanced views on politics and he also had great ideas how to overcome difficult situations. He became a great leader and master for young samurai just like Ryoma Sakamoto. But unlike Ryoma, who was challenging the Shogunate, Kaishyu held a high position in the Shogunate. When Ryoma Sakamoto met Kaishyu it was a turning point for all of Japan. They became partners to create a new avenue for reforming the country without war.

Kaishyu and Ryoma made a magnificent "bloodless revolution" happen in Japan.

Kaisyu made Ryoma the leader of his naval academy. The relationship between Ryoma and Kaishyu was a miracle. With Kaishyu's help and introductions, Ryoma met Takamori Saigou and other samurai leaders which led to an alliance with peace and unity rather than division and bloodshed. They were true warriors following the warrior's mission to fight to create peace.

"It is easy to 'destroy,' but it is difficult to 'create.' "

The crest of Kaishyu Katsu.

In 1860 Kaishyu under took a trip to the United States of America as a representative of the Japanese government on a ship called Irin Maru. His goal was to learn about Western society.

Kaishyu again showed that he was a true warrior with compassion as he sent sincere poems in honor of Ryoma Sakamoto and Takamori Saigo upon their deaths. With these poems and blessings Kaishyu showed strong love and respect for his former enemies who had become turned allies.

His beliefs and words:

"If someone tries to be famous, that is not easy. If someone wants to be a winner, that is not easy. We need to stand in a selfless space in our heart to accomplish goals."

"There is no class in occupation but there is class in how we live."

"The action belongs to myself. The criticism belongs to others and it's none of my business."

Shyoin Norikata Yoshida
吉田松陰-矩方 1830-1859

Honorific name: 烈 **Rage**
Sword name: 長船 **Osafune**

Shyoin was a great leader, revolutionary and educator. He was an amazing man who brought spirit back to the people of Japan during the late nineteenth century. He awakened people's hearts by sacrificing his own life. Shyoin was the great bridge between the older generation and the new. If we call Saigou Takamori and Ryoma Sakamoto heroes, then we could call Shyoin a hero maker.

Shyoin's philosophies carried into the modern era of the twentieth century as well. General Maresuke Nogi idolized Shyoin, and studied at the Shyoin School. Maresuke fought against Russia during World War II. He had much compassion in his heart and understood that war was an unfortunate action. Maresuke identified with the fact that the enemy were soldiers like himself who wanted to protect their loved ones. So he wanted to honor his enemy as well as his own troops. He built a monument in honor of the Russian troops he battled against before honoring his own troops. This action was carried down from the samurai code and Shyoin Yoshida's example.

Samurai would carry their own poem with them through their life and other samurai showed courtesy and respect by passing these poems on to their relatives.

Shyoin was placed under arrest after being caught attempting to board one of Commodore Matthew Perry's "black ships" anchored at Shimoda.

His last poem:

> *"Even when your body dies, the Yamato spirit* will live on."*
> 大和魂

* *The Yamato spirit is the pure Japanese spirit from ancient time.*

This last poem made a real impact on people, bringing them together during the country's crisis.

His beliefs and words:

> *"Once you set ambition, your heart's energy will be raised."*

> *"A wise man will act based on considering of logic. A stupid man will act based on considering benefit only."*

> *"Samurai will respect ethics, not talent. And respect action, not knowledge."*

The crest of Shyoin Yoshida.

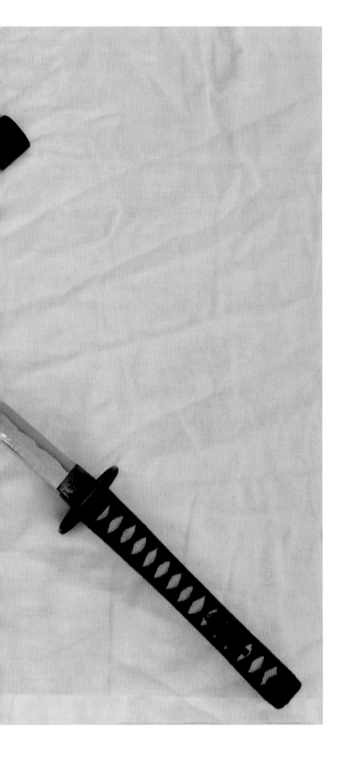

CHAPTER 3

THE
SAMURAI
SWORD

The ultimate enemy lies within us.

The sword is not just a weapon. It is a spiritual symbol used to fight and break your own weaknesses, negative energy and karma.

The samurai sword was originally a symbol standing for one's self-awareness, honor and dignity. Initially, it was not intended to be a weapon. In fact, after a long history of transformation and improvement for use as a weapon through the decades and centuries, the sword has returned to its original status as a symbol for spiritual warriors who are working for world peace. In ancient times the sword was born to help replace unclean energy with clean universal energy. The sword was like an antenna for the clean energy.

Japanese iron that will ultimately be refined to produce a sword.

TAMAHAGANE

This is a piece of iron rock called *tamahagane*. It will become a sword after it is forged and goes through the ceremony of the sword maker. The sword maker will use Shinto rites to produce each sword under a protective environment. Another term for *tamahagane* is *wako* meaning "Japanese iron."

Tamahagane comes from a specific type of iron ore that has a very low percentage of impurities. The sword maker purges any leftover impurities through a forging process to make the metal even more pure.

Getting Started

Since you are reading this book, you obviously have some sort of interest in or curiosity about the samurai sword. Developing an interest is but the first step. The next steps are learning the basic terminology about the sword, selecting a sword that is right for you, and learning to care for your sword. Let's begin.

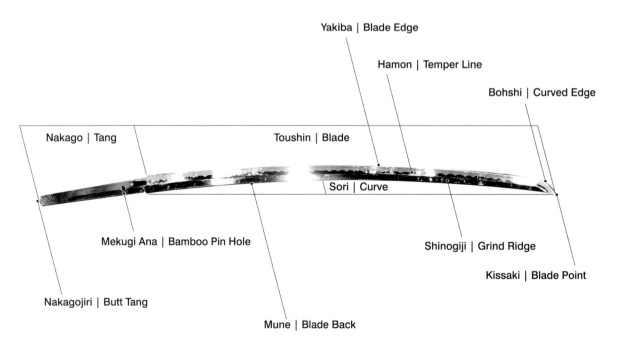

Samurai Sword Terminology

The original concept for a samurai sword was that it should be a two-handed sword, which was not commonly found in the time prior to the introduction of the samurai sword. However, the long, lightweight hilt made it easy to control the samurai sword with two hands.

KATANA

The *katana* or *daitou* sword is a long, single-sided blade with a slight curvature. With a double-handed grip added to the *katana*, the curved blade helps to make a clean cut.

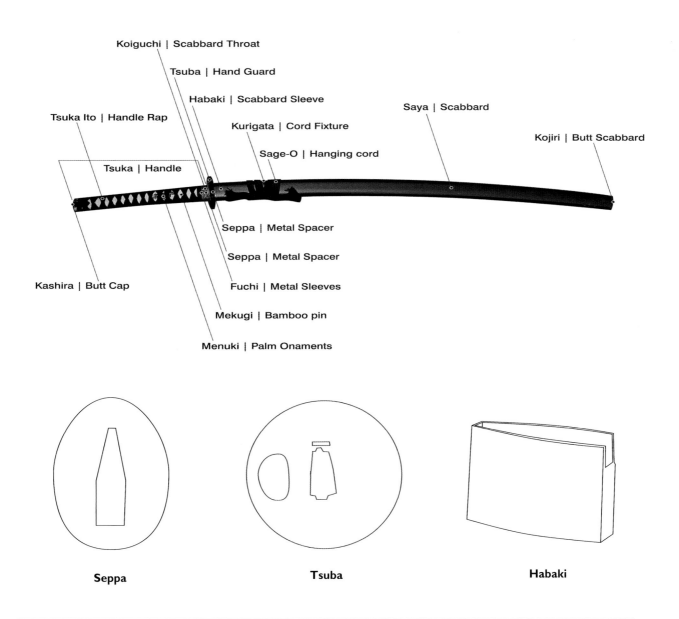

Seppa   Tsuba   Habaki

WAKIZASHI

The *wakizashi*, also known as *shyoutou*, was used as a spare for the *katana*. If the main sword was not in the right condition for use, the *wakizashi* was its backup and was also used as a dagger or tool in certain situations. In some instances, the two swords were used together. Musashi Miyamoto created a two-sword technique employing the *katana* and *wakizashi* together.

TACHI AND SHIRIZAYA

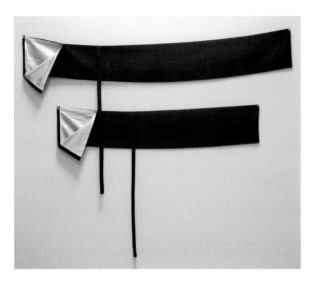

The *tachi* sword was designed for use on horseback. It was wider, had a more curved blade, and was heavier than the *katana*.

The *shirizaya* or scabbard was an ancient invention used to protect the *tachi*. Skins of boar, tiger or leopard were used as scabbards to prevent the sword from touching the horse and to protect it from rain and dew.

Many Japanese modern words are based on sword terms because the samurai sword is very much rooted in Japanese culture. Because of this, many people think and speak in sword terminology in the same way that many

Examples of modern shirizaya.

Americans use sports terminology. Moreover, many sword-related expressions have become part of everyday Japanese speech regarding decision-making or conscience.

Here are some interesting Japanese phrases using sword terminology:

SHINOGI WO KEZURU: You fight (struggle) so hard.

SEPPA TSUMARU: You lose your way trying to get out of a difficult situation.

MENUKI DOURI: A prosperous street.

SORI GA AWANAI: One's personality or character doesn't match another person's.

TSUBA ZERIAI: You cannot finish or resolve a situation easily.

Selecting and Maintaining Your Sword

First, one must select a sword. A new sword is preferable, if possible. Swords are great pieces of art that carry a human spirit very vividly. So the preference is to select a handmade sword because it carries the spirit of the sword maker. Or if you must select a used sword, you should try to find out about the previous owner if possible as the sword will carry the previous owner's spirit.

In modern times there is an exception as many swords are now made by machine. In this case, the sword obviously doesn't carry a swordmaker's spirit within it.

Many people, including myself, feel the sword is a mysterious object because it contains a human soul. The sword becomes almost a creature possessing its own will. This is based on the principle of *spiritual science*. This effect, called *nyu-kon*, means that one dedicates one's soul into a sword. The creator's vibration (thoughts and energy) will affect the sword. That is why if you choose a previously owned sword you should try to find out all you can about the previous-owner, when the sword was made, and the environment in which the sword was used. The previous owner's purpose in life remains with the sword, or more specifically the blade. The blade is the only part of the sword capable of taking in the vibrations of its maker and owner. So historical swords are absolutely not recommended for your personal collection. They should rest in a museum.

Wooden Practice Swords

Wooden practice swords (also known as *suburi-tou*) previously owned by someone else are a different story. These swords can be cleansed in an easy ritual such as burning the herb sage. Native Americans often use sage for cleansing objects.

Living as we do in a time of modern conveniences, it's always easy to visit your martial arts store to find a freshly manufactured wooden practice sword. In terms of quality, I recommend a heavier practice sword because it's closer in weight to a real sword in case you plan to learn to use a real sword in the future. Oak is used for many types of weapons. Likewise, oak tends to be a nice hardwood for a practice sword. In addition, it's best to have a *suburi-tou* with a standard *katana*-length shaft for realistic practice and to develop your body strength.

In general, a martial arts practitioner needs to be able to treat and feel all weapons as an extension of their body. If you have any spare time, carry it, swing the sword around with you, stretch with it and roll with it—just like the practitioner of any sport or trade. You may have heard that some people sleep with their tennis racquet or gun. A sword is the same. Begin to recognize the sword as part of your body and life. Starting out with this mindset is an enjoyable way to build enthusiasm and dedication as you make this practice a part of your life.

Selecting a Sword

Achieving the right balance of all conditions is the key. Good design and functionality are important when selecting the right sword for yourself. It's like finding a friend or partner. Select them as a human being, not as a thing or possession. Of course, the sharpness of the blade is important, as are the other physical properties. But here we will talk about the sword's design and beauty. This beauty is a natural process stemming from the process of its creation.

As far as design is concerned, a sword's beauty doesn't lie in a decorative hilt or scabbard. The beauty in the sword is expressed in the shape of the tip, or *kissaki*, and the curve of the blade. It's important to pay attention to the expression that shows up on the blade surface as specific waving or lines. Ultimately, the real value of the sword is the blade itself.

Here are some examples of distinctive designs to help you find the sword that is best for you:

KISSAKI: The Tip

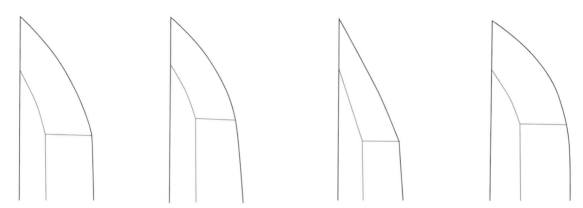

FUKURA: The Curve of the Tip

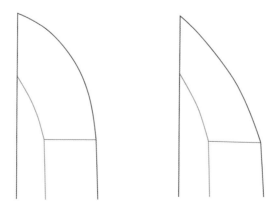

BOHSHI: The Wave on the Kissaki or Tip

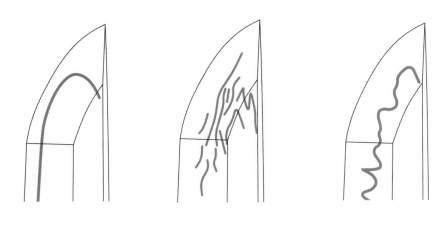

SORI: The Curve of the Blade

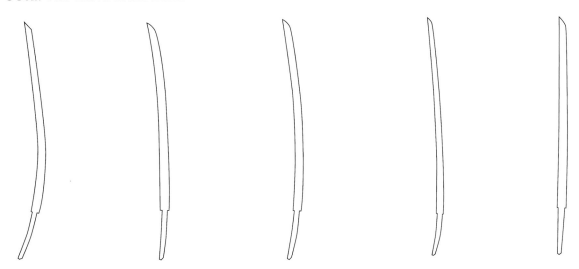

HAMON: The Wave on the Sharp Edge of the Blade

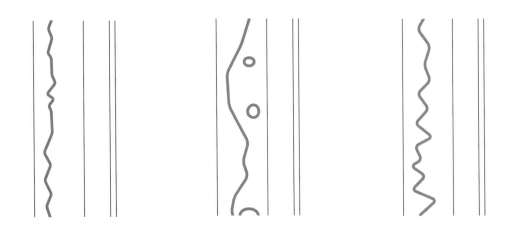

HI: The Line of the End of the Non-blade Side

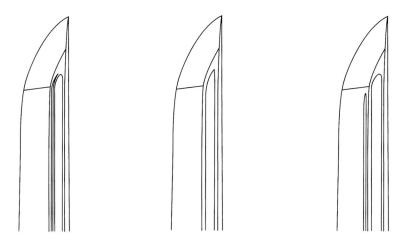

NAKAGO: The Hilt Section (that indicates the name of the sword and its maker).

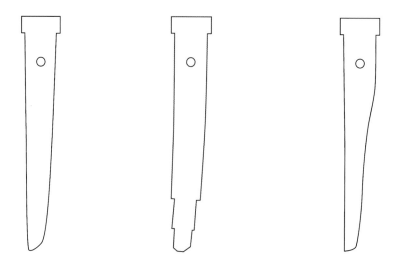

Once again, it's best if you know the sword maker or previous owner before selecting a sword so that you have an idea about the sword's history. However, learning about the sword maker can be challenging in modern times. So you may have to rely on only these physical characteristics to find the sword that is most pleasing to you. Analyzing a sword is like analyzing a piece of art in a museum. As you look at the characteristics, the piece takes on a life of its own in your perception and no two swords look alike. As you analyze the characteristics of a sword you must find one that you identify with. It's similar to building a relationship with a friend or a partner in life.

Cleaning Equipment

The following is a list of cleaning equipment that will help you to maintain your sword in top condition.

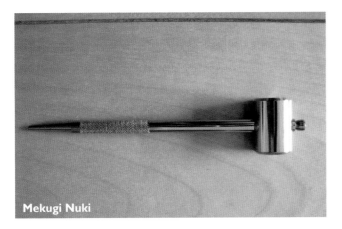

Mekugi Nuki

Uchiko

MEKUGI NUKI: A small pick for taking the *mekugi* (sword holder pin) out.

UCHIKO: An implement designed to dust cleaning powder onto a sword.

NUGUI GAMI (x2): Two cloths used to wipe powder and oil. One is for powder and one for oil. These are either made from fabric or a special paper specifically made for cleaning the sword. Tissue paper may also be used to take old oil off the blade, but it's best to use a very high quality paper for this.

It's good to have separate cloths for the blade and for the *nakago* near the hilt because the *nakago* tends to have rusty pieces that might come off on the cloth and scratch the blade.

Chyouji Abura

Nugui Gami

CHYOUJI ABURA: Oil to prevent the sword from rusting. This oil stops the oxidization process.

KEROSENE: If you leave *chyouji* oil on the blade too long it becomes a tough stain. Kerosene or lighter fluid will wash it off easily.

Cleaning Your Sword

1. Pull the sword out of the scabbard keeping the blade side (the sharp side), pointed up toward the ceiling. Handling the sword this way will help prevent the sword from getting scratched—it's also a safer way to handle the sword.

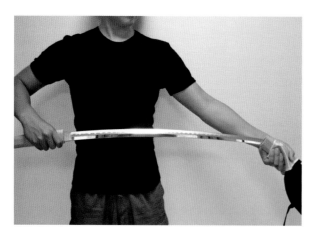 

2. First, hit the *mekugi* sword pin with the hammer, or head side, of the *mekugi nuki* pick lightly to loosen it for removal. You should hold the hilt in your left hand and use the *mekugi nuki* with your right hand to push the *mekugi* out from the hilt. Be careful not to lose the *mekugi*.

3. With the sword pointing upward, hold the *tsuka* (hilt) with your left hand. Use your right fist to hit your left wrist to jar the blade loose from the *tsuka*. Be careful so the blade doesn't shoot out of the *tsuka* suddenly. The blade will slowly lift up from the *tsuka* little by little with each hit. If you keep the blade at an upright angle, it will never lift out, so be sure to keep it tilted forward slightly.

If the blade and *nakago* are too tight, use the *kizuchi* (wooden mallet or hammer) and *ategi* (wooden hilt removal tool) to take the blade out.

4. You will take the *habaki* out. The *habaki* is a metal collar that surrounds the base of the blade. If the *habaki* is too tight, hold the *mune* (back of the sword) side of the *habaki* that you've covered with a cloth. Hit the cloth-covered part with the wooden hammer. The carefully applied force should take care of the tightness easily. If it's a sword with a *tsuba* (sword guard) and *seppa* (spacers—washers, in effect—that sandwich the *tsuba*), then you take them out at the same time.

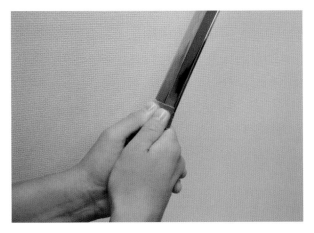

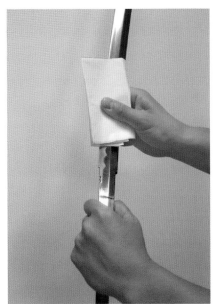

5. The next step is *nugui* (wiping). You should use two cloths or papers. If you're opting to use tissue paper, use lotion-free, high-quality tissue paper, as it's the softest kind. First, clean the dust and old oil from the blade. Wipe the blade from the *sori* (non-blade side) to make sure you don't cut your hand accidentally. Hold the blade from the *habaki* section and go all the way up to the tip. Don't hold too tightly. Hold and wipe the blade in a relaxed manner. Especially around the *mune* (back ridge) section, stay relaxed and follow the shape of the part.

6. Dust powder with the *uchiko* from the *habaki* section to the *shinogiji*, then flip the sword to the other side and do the same. You should also dust a little bit on the *mune* (ridge).

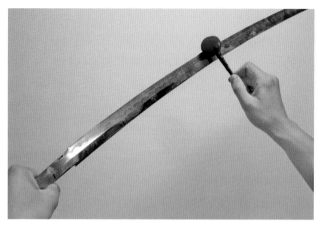

7. Use the second piece of paper to wipe all the powder off the blade following the same method as Step 5. Use the *nugui gami* or tissue to wipe the blade a few times to be sure it's clean and to see the hamon and other expressions on the blade. Now check for damage to the blade. Carefully check for any rust or chips on the blade. Then temporarily return the blade into the scabbard without the *habaki* back on it. It's good to keep track of which paper you used for each step for future use.

8. It's now time to prepare for rust prevention. Put oil onto a paper to wipe onto the blade starting from the *mune* side. You should make sure that you go little by little because too much oil on the blade may start dripping off and isn't good for the sword or the scabbard.

9. Put the *habaki*, *seppa*, *tsuba*, and other *seppa* back onto the hilt in that order. Hold the *tsuka* (hilt) at an upright angle and put the blade back into *tsuka*. Lastly, you will tap the very bottom of the *tsuka* as you are holding the sword at an upright angle to make sure the blade and *tsuka* successfully join again. Put the *mekugi* back into the tsuka to finish. Return the entire sword to its *scabbard*.

 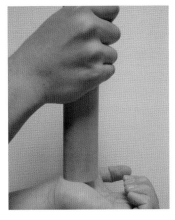 

The dismantling of the sword for a complete cleaning should be done every couple of months. As for daily cleaning, keep the sword in one piece and follow steps 5–8. The sword should be kept out of direct sunlight and in a dry place. This will help keep the sword in good condition and help extend the life of the sword.

Note: Keep your mouth closed by pressing your lips together on a Japanese paper called *washi* while you are doing the cleaning to prevent moisture from getting on the blade. Saliva on the blade is forbidden, so don't cough or spit during the cleaning process. Also, be sure to keep your hands dry so that sweat doesn't get on the blade.

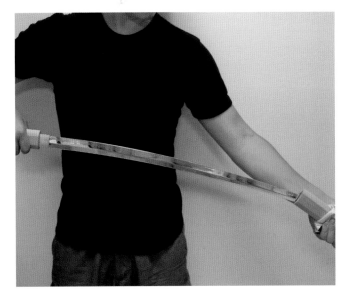

CHAPTER 4

BASIC TECHNIQUES

Practice with Faith

Have faith in yourself. Sometimes, many of us
fall off a cliff even though the beautiful sight
of a mountain is just one step ahead of us.
Enjoy your journey to taste that glory.

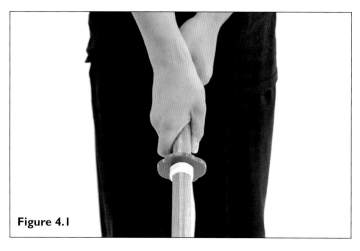

Figure 4.1

How to Grip the Sword

Knowing how to hold the sword properly is a significant achievement in itself. The left and right sides of the brain work together as do the left and right hands to create Yin and Yang power in the sword. In the principle of Yin and Yang, every action has a reaction. This principle is the essence of life itself. With regard to the sword, if the left hand is pulling, then the right hand is pushing, and vice versa.

1. The left hand holds the hilt near the bottom. This hand controls the movement of the sword, so keep a firm grip. The pinky and thumb should hold the sword more tightly than the other fingers, followed by the ring finger. The middle finger and index finger will have the loosest grip.

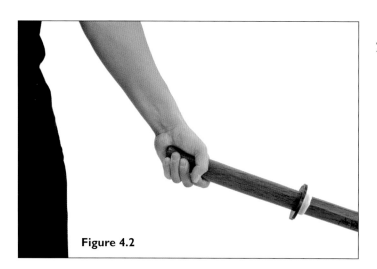

Figure 4.2

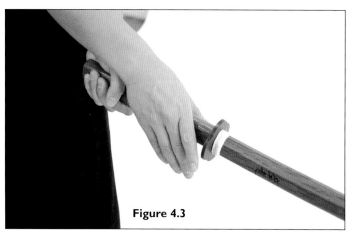

Figure 4.3

2. The right hand holds closer to the shield of the sword with a lighter grip than the left hand. The right hand is responsible for the power of the strike. This power doesn't mean that you have to hold the sword ferociously. In fact, the opposite is true. As you follow each movement and technique, the right hand should only squeeze at the last moment to create extra power—just like throwing a proper punch. See Figure 4.3. Both hands, especially the right, need to be diagonal when gripping the sword. This diagonal angle will keep the grip loose and the hands at the correct angle on the hilt. The blade should be facing toward the object that you are about to strike. It's very important to keep your wrists diagonal. If you hold the sword improperly, you can easily lose the right angle on the blade. This will cause the sword to bang and glance off the object rather than strike and cut into the object.

3. You can practice this proper grip position and
striking action by squeezing a piece of cloth
and imagining you are squeezing water out of
it. The left hand is pulling down and the right
hand is pushing at the same time. The hands are
squeezing together. While holding the sword,
keep your right wrist at a diagonal angle and keep
the blade at a right angle. This squeezing action is
the key. If you don't squeeze in the last moment,
you will lose control of the sword. Squeeze the
hilt nice and tight to keep the sword under

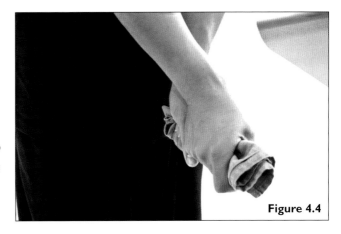

Figure 4.4

control. Keep your left hand about two fist-lengths away from your belly. Relax
your shoulders and neck. Keep your hands at your body's centerline and squeeze.
The goal is not to swing the blade straight down to the ground. You should strive
to move the sword at a downward angle away from your body.

How to Stand and Step

Your basic stance will be right foot
forward in a Walking Stance because
the right hand is in front when you
grip the sword. Your left heel should
be lifted slightly. When moving
forward, your right foot should step
first in a "step-and-slide" footstep with
the left foot sliding up into a Walking
Stance behind the right foot. Make
sure your left foot maintains contact
with the ground.

 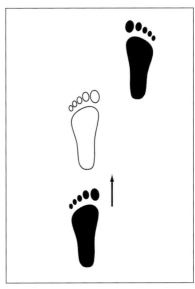

Figure 4.5

On the following pages you'll find a list of terms for the different positions. We'll
take you through the descriptions of each stance.

THE SEIGAN STANCE

Center of your body

Hold the sword tilted down almost parallel to the floor. The point of the sword should be angled up toward your opponent's throat. It's good to target the throat because you should avoid aiming too high and miss the head, which is very mobile. Since the throat is between the head and the body, it's a good place to aim. Since Seigan covers your centerline, it's great for both offense and defense.

Relax your shoulders and keep space between your body and arms and grip. You should keep a little space, about two fist-lengths between your belly and the bottom grip of the sword. Keep your elbows close to the body.

Figure 4.6

THE GEDAN STANCE

Low guard

Seigan in low position is Gedan. It looks defenseless compared to the basic Seigan position, but its potential depends on your intention. Gedan can be used for catching your opponent off guard or to defend against Daijyoudan, a downward strike.

Figure 4.7

THE DAIJYOUDAN STANCE

The overhead grip

Daijyoudan, the overhead grip, is a very aggressive position. Bring the sword straight up from the Seigan position with your hands above your head and you will be in Daijyoudan. Bend both elbows naturally and make sure your grip is tight. This grip will be unstable without bending your elbows properly. This is the ready position for Makkou, the downward strike, or for Kesa, the diagonal strike.

Figure 4.8

THE HASSOU STANCE

Sword on your right shoulder

The Hassou position can be very aggressive. It usually means you are ready for the Kesa slice. Some systems emphasize this position because it's much more efficient if you needed one shot to take care of your opponent. This right side set-up is more powerful than the reverse set-up with the sword chambered to the left shoulder. Due to the body mechanics, and your weight shift, the right side set-up makes it easier to strike. Keep the sword in the vertical position and squeeze the right hand tight, keeping it close to your right shoulder. The left hand is also tight and close to your chest. But don't lift your right shoulder unnecessarily.

Figure 4.9

Figure 4.10

THE REVERSE CHAMBER

All the same principles apply to the grip and arms as the regular right shoulder hold, but this side will generally be a weaker strike (unless you're left-handed). The Reverse Chamber is more useful between actions and in transitioning to another movement.

THE RELAXED HASSOU

Hold your sword in the same position as a regular Hassou. The difference is that you are more relaxed so there is extra space between your grip, chest and shoulder. The sword is also tilted backwards a little.

Figure 4.11   **Figure 4.12**   **Figure 4.13**

THE WAKI GAMAE STANCE

Sword at your right side on the hip bone

It might seem unwise to hold the sword behind you rather than keeping the blade closer to your opponent, however, the purpose here is to catch your opponent off guard. You are essentially hiding the sword blade from your opponent's sight. It's an advantage for you because you are withholding critical information from him regarding timing, length and distance. The length indicates the length of your sword. Keep the blade down toward the ground.

Figure 4.14

Figure 4.15

THE REVERSE WAKI GAMAE

The reverse Waki Gamae is an awkward technique. As with the Reverse Hassou grip, it's usually used when transitioning between positions.

TERMS USED FOR CUTTING LINES

The following are the terms for cutting lines:

- Makkou = vertical cut

- Kesa = diagonal cut

- Ichimonji = horizontal cut

- Kote = wrist cut

- Tsuki = stabbing cut

Each of the cutting lines shown below also has the equivalent action but in the opposite direction. For instance, the Makkou vertical cut can be made either downward or upward.

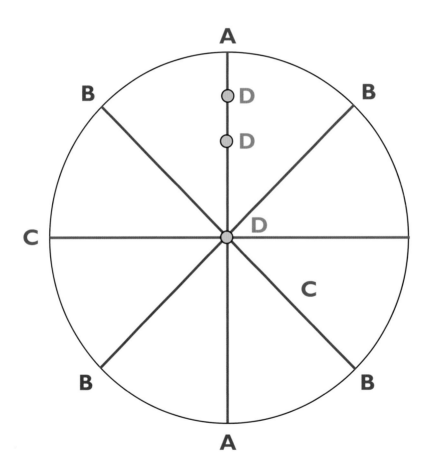

A. Makkou   **B. Kesa**   **C. Ichimonji**   D. Tsuki

TSUKI

Stabbing

Stabbing generally has three targets on the body. Low would be to the abdomen. Middle is to the chest. And high is to the throat. These targets are all on the torso because the head moves more easily which makes for a more difficult target to hit. Stabbing requires a technique of its own.

Figure 4.17

Please inspect Figure 4.17 carefully. You should push the sword with the left (back) hand, and the right hand is supporting that push. Both wrists' lines need to be straight. The line from the inward wrist to the thumb should be straight to keep your aim accurate. With this angle, stabbing will be more powerful and efficient. Though there are other body parts available as targets (head, arms, and legs) they tend to move which makes them more difficult to strike. The central body points are much more reliable places to aim. And if you can master striking these basic "D" spots (see the diagram in the sidebar) you will be able to go anywhere else you need to.

The center is steady and things will seek steadiness. Imagine a "pendulum." It will always seek the "center" during action. And humans have the same nature. It's called "seeking truth."

Basic Body Movements

❖ Basic Makkou vertical strike in the upright standing position.

Keep your right side forward. Advance with your front foot and drag your back foot. This advancing step should be about half your normal walking step length. Synchronize your striking action with your stepping. The very end of the striking moment and front step landing should be timed to match. You can either "cut in" (swing your sword downward and a little forward

Figure 4.18

Figure 4.19

Figure 4.20

Figure 4.21

diagonally at the same time) or "cut throw" (your sword will cut into the object and pass all the way through to the floor). As you advance, shift your body by dropping your hips and pulling your hands toward the chambered position (primarily use your upper body by turning and pulling the end of sword's hilt toward your hip— your left hand will pull with the most force). In this way, you are using the sword efficiently. Keep in mind that for other strikes or situations, your stance may vary.

❖ Same as the previous action but with a forward stance.

Bend your front knee to almost a 90-degree angle and keep your back knee almost straight (but don't lock your knee) to push and support your upper body action. This is more of a forward action, so it's a more aggressive stance. The blade can either cut into the target or slice through it.

❖ Cutting in a Makkou straight line and Kesa diagonal line.

The action of slicing through the object can be a more natural movement in this chambered position stance. This is because you are turning your left shoulder (or right shoulder) back toward the same side of your hip, so it naturally draws your sword in a diagonal angle. This diagonal angle is called Kesa. This term came from the proper dress of the Buddhist monk called "Kesa." The monastic garment is designed to hang from one shoulder to cover all your body below the chest. This Kesa cloth hanging naturally from the shoulder draws a beautiful diagonal line from one shoulder to the other side of the rib cage.

Similarly, the Kesa cut means to slice in from one shoulder through the rib cage on the other side.

The term Makkou means absolutely straight down the center.

❖ Train your lower body by repeating a steady swinging action back and forth with the sword.

This will also teach you basic steady-armed movement for any stance you may use in any situation. Match your swing and step. Exaggerate a wide stance with overhead swinging action both to the left and the right. This movement essentially applies to Kesa (diagonal-line). Practice this action, being aware that it can be useful for both offense and defense at the same time. This overhead swinging action could turn into a "roof block" that covers your head area. You will read more about the roof block in Chapter 6, *Kata Practice*.

1. Begin in an exaggerated wide stance in a reverse guard with your weapon pointed low on your left side.

Figure 4.22

| Figure 4.23 | Figure 4.24 | Figure 4.25 |

2. Step forward with your left foot and bring the sword overhead into an upper-level guard.

3. Bring the sword down in a diagonal cut to the right.

4. Complete the diagonal cut to the right.

5. Return the sword to an upper-level guard.

Figure 4.26

Figure 4.27   **Figure 4.28**

6. This time bring the sword down in a diagonal cut to the left.

7. The exercise is now complete. Repeat this exercise often to train your body. This versatile movement can be used in many situations and contains a good mix of offensive and defensive elements.

❖ Practice the proper positions by repeating them in the same sequence until they become second nature.

Traditional Stance

1. Keep your feet shoulder width apart with your back straight and shoulders relaxed. Keep your chin down near your throat. And stay rooted to the ground with your feet. Focus on your abdomen to solar plexus to settle your weight and energy. Don't breathe with your shoulders. You should breathe deeply from your abdomen to balance your internal energy. Breathe in and out through your nose. Repeat a few times to make sure you are focusing.

Figure 4.29

2. Draw your sword

Figure 4.30

3. Overhead

4. Arching strike

Figure 4.31

Figure 4.32

5. Retreat step holding your sword at the right shoulder

Figure 4.33

6. Advancing step with a diagonal slice downward

Figure 4.34

7. Half-step retreat, neutral hold

Figure 4.35

8. Left shoulder hold

Figure 4.36

9. Horizontal slice with stepping in

Figure 4.37

10. Reverse horizontal slice with
advancing step

Figure 4.38

Figure 4.39

Figure 4.40

11. Reverse left chamber hold

12. Diagonal upward cut with advancing step

13. Place the sword back into scabbard

As you get more comfortable and confident with these positions you will speed up or slow down on some particular movements on purpose to find what is the best timing and relaxation for you in the specific moment. You may understand from playing other sports about being "off rhythm" or "off timing." You will find your own comfort zone as you practice.

Figure 4.41

CHAPTER 5

STRIKING TECHNIQUES

Striking is just like spreading your wings. In life, we are always reaching out to the sky, striking for something: dreams, glory, goals or a better tomorrow. Developing precision in your striking techniques is a very important step toward mastery of the samurai sword. This has very much to do with your aiming ability, so this practice will sharpen your vision and accuracy. As you train, you can also expect to see improvements in your physique. Continue to practice these techniques so that they become second nature.

Figure 5.1   **Figure 5.2**

The Vertical Strike Using an Advancing Step

Maintain the basic Walking Stance throughout the exercise. Start with the sword
in the overhead position. Move forward with the Advancing Step (front foot step
a few inches forward with rear foot following—almost like a hop—ending in the
Walking Stance) and strike downward to the neutral position. Then move back with
the Retreating Step (reverse of Advancing Step) while returning the sword to the
overhead position. Repeat this forward and backward technique to establish your
striking coordination and build your body strength at the same time. Don't forget
to squeeze your grip as you strike. If you don't synchronize the timing for your
squeezing and advancing, your footwork will get ahead of your hands. Synchronize
your body movement and breathing. Strike with an exhalation and inhale while
swinging upward.

Figure 5.3

Figure 5.4

The Horizontal Diagonal Strike at Head Level

Strike in a diagonal line at the head of your target. In the beginning it's good to just do the striking motion without footwork. As the striking motion becomes more comfortable, add the advancing footstep. Bring or swing the sword above your head in a circular motion as the set-up for the diagonal cut. If you are cutting downward from right-to-left you should lift the sword to the left and bring it around your head into the diagonal line from your upper right down to your left. Lift to the right to prepare for a left-to-right cut. Be sure to cut with the body of the blade and not just the kissaki point. Aim for the opponent's temple, neck, or collarbone.

Actions with Two Swords

You can strengthen your coordination and strength by using double swords as in Figures 5.5–5.8. Use the swords by holding the pointed end rather than the hilts because wooden practice swords are made with the hilt heavier than the blade end. So if you use them in this manner they will provide a good weight with which to train your body. You can practice swinging the sword at any angle or body position for this drill. These pictures show the horizontal or diagonal strike from head level.

Keeping your right foot forward, use a Walking Stance with the advancing step while striking. Try the same drill, but with the shuffle step and with any other movement. Be creative with your combinations.

Figure 5.5

Figure 5.6

Figure 5.7

Figure 5.8

Walking Through with a Stabbing Action in the Down Position

One usually doesn't use stabbing action by itself in a given situation—it becomes useful in between other movements. This training position can be tough for the body, but it teaches us how to deal with small spaces with the long sword. The long sword is not designed for small spaces, but this stabbing action is very useful because you are dealing with limited space by applying the concept of a point rather than a line. This is also a very good exercise for training your body (especially the lower body)—it's good for your sense of balance as well. Certain sections of the human brain tend to sleep, so wake them up by using martial arts practice for mental exercise as well.

Figure 5.9

While in your normal Walking Stance, simply squat straight down. Don't let your back knee touch the ground. Staying on the ball of your foot will help with this. Your center of gravity should be straight down through your tailbone to the ground so that you are not off balance as you step. Keep your sword in front of your belly with a two-fist space as usual. Keep your shoulders and neck relaxed. Pull the sword to your chambered position as you turn the blade outward by turning your wrist and right hand up to the ceiling. This motion is just like the action of pulling rope in to your side. When you pull your arms in, the tip of the sword should still be connected to the central line created between you and your target.

Figure 5.10

As you step up (without lifting your body up), stab your sword in front. Be clear what you are aiming at with your imaginary target. If you have a partner, it makes it easier to aim. But for solo training, use your imagination vividly. Don't lift your shoulders too high as this will tense your muscles and it will cause you to fall or throw off your balance. If you have to really reach forward, then you might have to use a landing step so you don't open your body in an unguarded way.

Figure 5.11

Figure 5.12

This action should get your entire body moving and not only your feet and arms. Turn your front shoulder in and push your back shoulder forward as you stab while stepping up—like a compact tornado to create quick impact with the sword. Be careful that the point of the sword is not leaning over too much because this will diminish the strength of the impact. Don't let your head bob up and down while stepping. Keep your head level during the entire action.

As you get comfortable with the advancing movement, be sure to practice retreating as well. If you can practice this with a partner one of you will advance while the other retreats. Your swords should meet in the center.

Figure 5.13

Figure 5.14   Figure 5.15

The Single-handed Swing

Grab the tip of the sword in order to use the weight from the hilt, or heavier side of
the sword. This will teach you to control the sword and will help to build specific
muscle groups in your forearms and shoulders. It's important to make the swinging
action from both the shoulder and the wrist. This will build different areas of control
and strength. If you train both arms equally this single hand swinging action will
help us to stay well balanced with equal strength in both arms. The action here
is more like throwing a sword than striking with it. Though you are training for
striking you are also training to control the sword, and in this drill you will have
the feeling of throwing the sword. If you swing the sword with the intent to cut or
strike, your sword will tend to accelerate in the last moment before it stops. Focus
on feeling the difference between "reaching out" and "striking downward." Reaching
out will train your forearms and shoulders in different ways.

Figure 5.16　　　　　　**Figure 5.17**

First practice the single-handed swing without footwork. Then, as you become more comfortable, you can start to use the regular footwork of switching your front leg forward and backward as you strike. Your striking hand and stepping foot need to be synchronized because the footwork will cause your center of gravity to shift and thus lend more power to the strike. This factor should give you more incentive to develop proper timing.

You can also try switching to opposite leg positions (crossing leg) in synchronization with your striking hand. This will provide a good opportunity to become more comfortable with an awkward position, and to produce proper power (effectiveness) without being limited by body position. It's also good to experiment with different rhythms and different footwork will produce different rhythms.

At the next level you can try to play with different body positions and footwork. Try a forward or front stance rather than a Walking Stance. Or stay in a lower position the entire time. And, if you want to add more work for yourself, swing the sword in a circular motion before throwing or striking. This will be good for your body /brain coordination and, more importantly, it will teach you how to maintain a quiet spirit even as your body is making rapid movements.

Figure 5.19

Figure 5.18

Figure 5.20

Quick Repetitions on Both Sides

In this practice exercise, you will use a lot of up and down motion to establish flexible coordination. You move between extra "looseness" and "tension in momentum." Your entire action should be drawing a circle with your sword.

a. The Shoulder hold

This position, called the Hassou, is a very aggressive position. You squeeze the sword hilt to your right shoulder or chest to set it very tightly. The tip of the sword points straight up to the sky or you can take a modified position with the tip tilted slightly behind you. The tightness in this grip is firm enough that, even if you start to run, the sword should stay in place.

b. Squat down as you release your hold and you are ready to sweep (strike) the leg.

When you squat down, use your weight and gravity to go just straight down to ground. In other words, let your weight drop without exertion.

c. Rise up cutting from the leg to the body.

Cut into the line before you stand up again. As you see it in Figure 5.20, you should swing the sword upward before standing up. As soon as you finish the cutting action, stand and return your sword to the other shoulder in the reversed Kesa position. Make sure that you cut with the blade because, if you are not paying attention, the sword can turn and you could end up hitting a target instead of cutting it.

Figure 5.21

Figure 5.22

d. Strike horizontally to the head

From your standing position with the reversed Hassou position you keep the flow of the swing and turn your hips into the next position for a reverse horizontal cut. Don't swing the sword all the way behind you. You are not swinging the sword like a baseball bat.

e. Bring the sword back to the original shoulder hold.

Work to get quicker and more relaxed as you get used to this drill. Try this drill on both sides. You should be making a circular movement but it's actually more of a diagonal circle as shown in the diagrams on the opposite page. You can practice one action at a time with separate breathing and as you get comfortable finish the whole action with fewer breaths. Your main focus should be to build proper techniques. As your technique improves, the speed of the technique will follow.

Figure 5.23

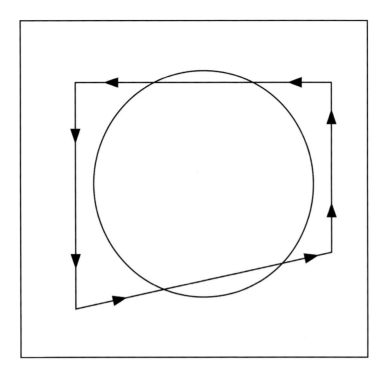

Figure 5.24

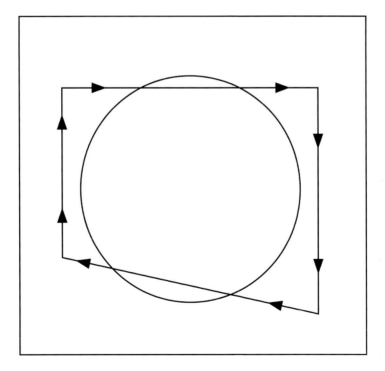

Figure 5.25

CHAPTER 6

KATA PRACTICE

The samurai way calls for you to answer another person's hearts with your own heart. As a teacher I want to make sure that I am sincere and hold great love in my heart because my students are opening themselves up and trusting me to guide them. I will reward that trust with a pure heart. That is called honor.

Kata literally means "form" in Japanese. The purpose of the kata is to repeat the same sequence of actions in the same order over and over again to establish a certain amount of coordination and to understand its principles. One form or another of this disciplined practice can be found in all the martial arts.

As you get more comfortable with the sequence of movements in the kata you can start to create your own rhythms in different sections. Find different ways to use the techniques and determine how the changes affect you. Develop versatility, because a real battle always provides you with very different spontaneous situations—just like in your regular life. You need to be flexible in mind and body to succeed.

While breaking down movements you can see how a defensive movement can be turned into an offensive technique, and vice versa. But please don't rush! It's very important to keep your feet on the ground and develop solid fundamentals. This process is called 守破離 **Shyu Ha Ri**. This is the term for the process of development and growth. It defines that very gradual way that one evolves without getting lost in the process. If you don't forget about this process, you can be an upstanding and respectable individual who possesses both good techniques and a good heart at the same time. This mirrors the same growth process that you observe in other aspects of your life. That is why the practices of the martial arts mirror the ways of human kind.

As mentioned, 守破離 **Shyu Ha Ri** represents the core concept for a practitioner's journey. This key phrase is broken down in the following sections.

SHYU

To Protect

The straight translation of "*shyu*" is to protect. The idea is that you will show the commitment that is necessary for you to follow what your instructor or parents are going to teach or provide. You will study the curriculum or program without any doubt or resistance. Expand your heart's capacity to accept this value system and this acceptance will help to erase war and conflict from this world. In other words, you will put your feet into other people's shoes to understand their feelings, ideas, and education. So in this stage you will study how to wear those shoes and walk around in them without complaining. This stage is comparable to childhood.

破 HA

To Break

The straight translation of "*ha*" is to break. Though you start to discover your favorite tastes you still follow your teacher. You can start to play with different ideas that you come up with, but you should not depart from your instructor's teachings yet. You are allowed to make modifications to traditional doctrines in your own way to see how it's going to work as well as continue to follow your teacher's lead. At this point you should work on being creative and thinking on your own, but you can also ask for help and support whenever you need to do so. You still have a solid foundation that you can fall back on. This second stage would be equivalent to the teenage years.

You are beginning to open up your personality to try to find your individuality. But as one sees in the process, parents still have to watch very carefully to make sure that the teenager doesn't stray from the proper path. It might be a tough time for both sides, but it's also a good challenge for instructors and parents to grow into a higher level as a mentor.

離 RI

To Depart

The straight translation of "*ri*" is to depart. Eventually you need to stand up on your own feet. Now you become very responsible and develop an existence where others might come to you to ask your help and support. Your mentor wants to bless your journey now. You will create your own way to raise followers even as you continue to hold great respect for your senior. The cycle continues with your students and so on as that heart will be passed on and on, forever. Do not break this chain— maintain the tradition. No matter how much one changes and evolves in the future this tradition will continue. Respect, appreciation and love are paid to teachers by passing on their philosophies to your own students. This third stage is equivalent to becoming an adult and entering society as a responsible individual. Your main job is to create a better world by creating a great family or great juniors as well as taking care of your seniors. This activity creates a beautiful world. And that is why I also respect a martial artist who possesses a healthy personality that goes beyond simply emphasizing their skills. Passing your good spirit to the next generation is the best reward for your instructor and parents. And that is lineage.

Some of us will take more time in the first stage and others will take more time in other stages, but that is to be expected, as we are all different individuals.

Each process has a different feeling to you because you are evolving with it. The kata practice should not be just wandering around. It carries spirit within it and there should always be a purpose.

型 KATA

Figure 6.1

Let's begin the kata practice.

1. Standing in a neutral position.

Make your feet shoulder width apart with your knees slightly bent to keep them loose. Your shoulders should be relaxed. Your central weight is pulled straight down to the ground by an imaginary line connecting through your tailbone. Your sword is attached to your hipbone as you keep the blade side up toward the sky and the tip is tilted down to the ground. Your left thumb is set right on the shield or about to push the shield up to draw the sword out. Your right arm is slightly bent with your right hand making a little diagonal circle by engaging the index finger and thumb as they keep a little space between them to relax the grip. Take a few breaths keeping your mouth closed. Inhale through the nose and exhale through the mouth for deeper breaths. Focus on your first chakkra below your belly button. As you repeat this breathing, it will create quick energy flow inside your body. When you feel your energy is ready draw your sword out slowly with a deep breath.

2. Battou: Taking the sword out of its sheath

Step forward two steps, starting with left foot and then the right, pulling sword out of the scabbard while stepping with the right foot into a neutral back stance. When stepping with your left foot you should not turn your body. Rather, you should keep your body facing forward and use a dragging step with your left foot, keeping it in contact with the ground.

Figure 6.2

Breaking these movements down will include a traditional method called IAI. While stepping forward, with your left foot out of the neutral stance, you will use your left hand (holding the scabbard) to turn the scabbard (blade) outward away from your body. As you turn the scabbard, keep your left thumb on the guard of the sword pushing the sword out of the scabbard slightly. At this moment you should simultaneously grab the hilt of the sword with your right hand. Be sure to hold the hilt loosely until the moment you pull the sword out of its scabbard.

As you take the second step with your right foot you will draw the sword out of the scabbard into a horizontal slice from one side of the ribcage to the other. As you pull the sword out you will squeeze the hilt. Your grip and arm actions are working in concert to make the sword's curving action from blade to tip for a proper slice. Exhale during this movement, but don't open your mouth wide while breathing because you need to control your breaths. Your breath needs to originate from close to your stomach for proper energy and power.

3. Take two advancing steps with a downward slash.

Figure 6.3

Step forward two steps into another open stance while raising the sword above your head and slashing downward. (Beginners can actually omit the two steps and just do the slash. You can try the double step when you get a little more comfortable later on.) Without the footsteps, the beginner may simply lift the sword over his or her head and make your slicing motion downward. If you're including the footsteps, synchronize your lifting the sword above your head with the footsteps and the downward slash with your open stance. Keep your head level and your body under control because the footsteps are a dynamic action. Your drawing line will follow a curved path. This is a natural and effective line for the samurai sword because of the curve in the blade design. You should pull the sword back and toward yourself as you cut downward.

As you make your cut, sink your body weight down as you pull the sword back for the completion of the cut. In doing this every section of the sword will contact the target naturally for an efficient cut. See Figure 6.4 for proper body position at the end of the striking motion.

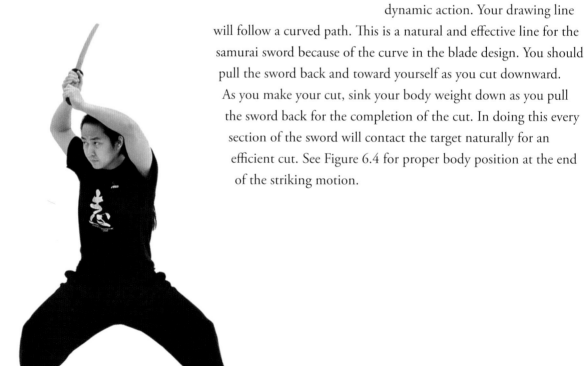

Figure 6.4

4. Turn back in the opposite direction.

Turn left 180 degrees and slide or re-adjust your left foot to the left so that you have an open stance facing the opposite direction without being off balance. As you turn you don't adjust how you are holding the sword. This holding position, as seen in Figure 6.5, is called Waki-Gamae. This means holding a sword on the side. In Waki-Gamae, you need to hide your sword from the opponent, so hide your blade behind your body.

5. Cutting up with an advancing step.

Begin lifting your sword forward as you step forward with your right foot with an upward vertical cutting line. This is a reversed Makkou cutting line. Synchronize your sword action and footstep. And be sure that you begin to raise your sword before stepping to avoid the risk of cutting your own foot or heel if the sword is behind your footstep. Also, it will be predictable to your opponent if you step first. Your stance is not quite a traditional forward stance. Your body is leaning forward to reach your target, but don't be stiff.

One optional step 5 substitution is a stabbing technique rather than the upward slice.

Figure 6.5

Figure 6.6

Figure 6.7

Figure 6.8

Figure 6.9

Figure 6.10

For this alternative move, slowly bring the sword up behind your shoulder in a slow 1-2 count. This becomes a modified Hassou position holding the sword above your shoulder. As you bring the sword up turn the tip of the sword to aim it at your opponent. When the sword sits on your right shoulder, the blade is turned to the sky. Quickly step forward with your right leg, stabbing and twisting the sword at the same time in a quick compact action. When you complete the stab with your arms extended completely, you should see your wrists flat and straight, reaching toward the target. (See Figure 6.10)

Figure 6.11

6. A quick reverse turn with a downward cut.

Keep the sword held high as you turn left to look behind you while sliding your left foot over so you can turn 180 degrees again (back to the direction you started the kata). Slice straight down from your opponent's head to toe with a vertical Makkou cutting line while dropping your right knee to the ground.

Figure 6.12

7. Rise up as you make an escape step with an upward block.

Rise up quickly as you are making an escape step to the side with your left foot. As you step, look to your right and bring the sword up to cover the right side of your head with a "roof block." This block should not need to take 100% of the impact from the opponent's strike because you have escaped partly with your side step and also from tilting your body to the opposite side. In addition, your sword also should be tilted downward slightly to deflect the impact from the opponent's offensive. Just be sure that your hands and sword are higher than your head so that you don't get cut. Another reason you should strive for a glancing blow rather than full contact is that the sword can easily be damaged with a strong impact. You need to maintain the integrity of the sword to be able to continue the battle.

Figure 6.13

Figure 6.14

Figure 6.15

8. The downward block

Because your roof block from step 7 has let your opponent's sword slide down your sword, it is easy for your opponent to quickly attack your lower body. So you need to cover your lower body (legs) immediately. As you keep your body tilted from the roof block, bring the sword down for a downward block immediately without taking a step. This downward block is in a reversed front stance in order to keep your lower body from being a good target. Keep your blade away from your body for a measure of safety. If the blade is too close to your body, for instance, if you are being timid, you will increase the potential of getting cut. Keep a decent amount of space around you and the blade both in front and to the side to block.

Figure 6.16   **Figure 6.17**

Figure 6.18

9. A reverse turn with an inside downward block.

This is a single-handed block, so it's not a strong block. You should be able to step around your opponent's strike. The purpose here is to invite your opponent to attack so that you may counterattack. You need to stay flexible and parry the attack. If the strike is too strong, your staying loose and flexible will enable you to step around the attack as well.

Another opponent is attacking from your left. Make a semi-circular turn to the left by stepping all the way around to the opposite side of your downward block with your right foot. At the same time bring your sword around keeping the tip pointed straight down. Also, your right elbow needs to stay bent to bring the sword around in a circular motion and keep space between the blade and your body. Your right hand is holding the sword and comes around in a modified hook punch motion with your palm facing outward. Because you are stepping and turning you are using your entire body for the block rather than just your arm movement. The whole circular movement is what makes the block work. Also, remember that you are only trying to deflect the attacker's sword—not strike it.

Figure 6.19

Figure 6.20   **10.** A downward block turning into a diagonal slice

Use the impact from the inside downward block to turn your sword into Kesa
position immediately. This action should be so well rehearsed that is seems
to happen by instinct. Use the strong rebound from the impact of the inside
downward block to automatically flip your sword away. Your wrist is going to
make a very small turn by using this rebound that will cause your thumb to
turn upward. You don't have to go around over your head to potentially lose this
opportunity to make a good counter action. Bringing the sword over your head
may take too long. Sink your body down as you slice. Because you don't have the
time to make a big swing, use your weight shift to make the diagonal slice from
your opponent's clavicle to the opposite ribcage.

Figure 6.21

11. Stabbing

Pull the butt of the sword hilt back quickly to your midsection as soon as you finish your Kesa cut. Step into a forward stance with your right foot to make a strong thrust and stab with the tip of your sword. Be sure to stab as you step into the forward stance.

Figure 6.22

12. The Daitou (end): Put your sword back into its sheath.

Step back with your right foot to your neutral stance, facing forward as you put the sword back into its scabbard. Take a deep, cleansing breath to return to a state of calm.

Figure 6.23

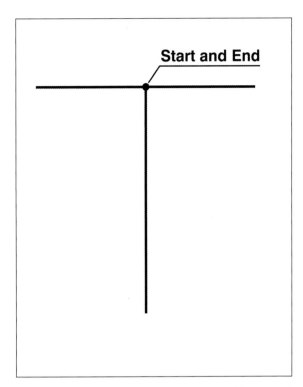

Figure 6.24

Movements 1–6 occur on the same line and 7–11 on a perpendicular line.

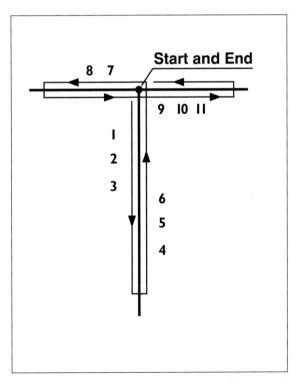

This diagram shows which direction you should be moving for each movement. The kata should start and end in the same spot.

Figure 6.25

CHAPTER 7

ADVANCED TECHNIQUES

*Your spear goes against your own shield—
the battle is a beautiful contradiction.*

Partner Drills

In the beginning of your training you found good *Yin* & *Yang* in how you grip the sword, your body coordination and in the principles of your basic techniques. And now you are going to find even better harmony in working with a partner. The contradiction of "your spear goes against your own shield" is called *Mu Jyun* in Japanese. The concept here is to learn how to deal with fighting. The contradiction is that we know that fighting is not good, yet we need to have conflicts to refine ourselves.

矛盾

Paradox. Mastering one's heart is to find miraculous balance within it.

The word *arigatou* means "thank you" in Japanese. But "arigatou" includes a word within it that means "difficulty" or "trouble." So literally you are expressing appreciation for the conflicts that are brought to you.

Work well with your partner and you can uplift each other. This is a wonderful principle that is applicable to many areas of life.

Defending against a Vertical Cut

The *Makkou* (vertical) position is very common and is an aggressive movement.

Figure 7.1

Figure 7.2

Defending with a Horizontal Slice

The opponent is coming straight at you with a *Makkou* (vertical) cut and you step forward at a diagonal angle to your right as you counter with a horizontal cut to your opponent's stomach. The diagonal step is already saving you from the vertical cutting line as you are stepping out of the strike zone. This defense depends on distance. If the attack is not deep enough, which means the opponent doesn't step far enough into your range, then you would choose another action for your counter. But if the opponent moves in close enough you can safely counter with this technique. Make sure you look back and turn around to once again face your opponent right after passing each other. And as you turn back to your opponent, point the tip of your sword toward them immediately. This is a precaution in case your opponent manages to recover quickly enough to continue to press the attack.

Figure 7.3

An Upward Block Turning into a Diagonal Slice

Use the same footwork as you did with the horizontal slice defense discussed earlier in this chapter. Step forward at a diagonal angle to your right as you lift the sword into an upward block or roof block. Lift your hands upward to the right side of your head leaving the blade above your head and angled with the tip pointed downward to your left. You will receive the opponent's strike as a parry or deflection rather than taking the full impact of the attack. As I mentioned in the discussion of the basic *kata*, you need to deflect the blow so that the opponent's sword slides down your sword rather than damaging it. Also, taking the full force of the attack may inhibit your next movement or counter move.

After deflecting the initial attack, immediately step to your right and turn toward your opponent. As you turn you should flip your sword over your head into position for a diagonal slice starting at your opponent's neck.

In an actual conflict in old Japan this would be the perfect moment to ask for your opponent's surrender. It would not be appropriate to go straight for the finish. In the samurai warrior way, it would be compassionate to ask for your opponent's surrender.

Figure 7.4

Figure 7.5

Figure 7.6

Knock your Opponent's Sword down and Return to the Offense

This is an essential technique for the advanced student. You must use your mind as well as your body to perform to the best of your abilities. Your mind needs to dance in the moment of your opponent's attack. In this scenario you need to have proper timing in order to knock your opponent's sword away.

Like the previous techniques, take a forward diagonal step to the right. The most important part of the technique is to avoid the attack. As you avoid, swing your sword left to knock your opponent's sword away. You are actually swinging over your opponent's sword and knocking it on the *mune* side, or non-blade side, of the sword.

This is a timing technique as your opponent is swinging downward quickly. If you don't hit your opponent's sword, don't worry. Again, the most important thing is to avoid the attack by moving out of the way. But if your counter-knock is successful, use the rebound to mount a counter-offense at your opponent.

After knocking your opponent's sword, step in with your left foot while bringing your sword upward into a diagonal slice at your opponent's throat line.

Figure 7.7

Figure 7.8

Figure 7.9

Making a Circle Step to Counter from the Waki Gamae Position

Step diagonally to your left with your left foot and turn your body slightly. If you need to do so repeat the step to stay to the outside shoulder of your opponent. Because you are circling to the outside of your opponent's lead hand and leg, you are generally in their blind spot. As you step to your left, drop your sword to your right side with your hands at your waist level. Your choices of counter-attacking are either an upward reversed diagonal cut from the opponent's ribcage to their shoulder or a horizontal slice across the torso.

Figure 7.10

Figure 7.11

Defending against a Diagonal Cut

The diagonal cut is very common and natural for many. It's a very fast and aggressive attack similar to *Makkou*. In this section both parties are holding the sword in *Hassou* (diagonal) position above the right shoulder.

Receive the Sword and Push It back with a Body Tackle

As your opponent begins their attack you must advance quickly, keeping your elbows in close to your body so that you maintain control of your sword. You should crash your opponent's sword back at them while maintaining strong tension in your arms to keep your opponent off balance and moving backward. You should be

Figure 7.12

able to cut your opponent if necessary, but they shouldn't be able to cut you as you keep your sword above your opponent's. Some technical advice: Don't raise your arms too high to push. Keep your sword and arms extended, but use your body and breathing like an air compressor in your stomach as you execute a very short and

Figure 7.13

Figure 7.14

Figure 7.15

explosive push rather than using muscle strength alone to struggle in the situation. Maintaining this tension will allow you to create space for your next movement or you can retreat, if necessary, as you've already made a separation.

With a larger or heavier opponent, you have another option besides just trying to push them backward. Your other option would be to step around your opponent or sweep his leg by stepping in behind his leg as you keep your sword firm.

Defending against a Horizontal Cut

This horizontal line tends to come from the *Waki Gamae* position and it can be a difficult one to see.

Left Hand Single Hand Counter to the Wrist

You need to carefully watch your opponent's shoulder movement since their sword is not in a visible position (*Waki Gamae*). You will escape to a safe zone by making a big round step to your left where the attack is coming from. If you escape to your right, you are following the cutting path and it's not a safe and economical choice for your movement.

Figure 7.16

Figure 7.17

Be sure to step to your left (not forward) and let the opponent's sword pass in front of you. Stepping to the left takes you to your opponent's blind spot and makes it more difficult for them to make another cut at you.

As you're completing your escape step, swing your sword down to the opponent's wrist. This is a one-handed (left hand) cut as you are moving far enough away from your opponent to be safe, yet remain able to reach your opponent's wrist.

Knock the Opponent's Sword down and Counterattack

This technique is power against power. You are using force to kill force instead of parrying or deflecting the attack with an angle step or turn. This is an "impact" technique. It's not the best choice of defense, but it will work if you don't have enough time or space to otherwise deal with the attack.

In this instance, while your opponent attacks from *Waki Gamae* with a horizontal slice, you are in the *Daijyoudan* position with the sword above your head. As the opponent steps in for the attack, you step back with your left foot to keep a good distance between you and your opponent as you bring your sword down in a vertical slice on top of the attacker's sword. This will also help to make your downward strike stronger.

Be sure to watch your opponent's step and arms and shoulders to judge the timing of his attack. Watching for just his sword movement may allow you to make a critical

---

Figure 7.18

Figure 7.19

timing error, as the sword movement is very fast. Watching his arms and shoulders carefully is the key to intercepting the attack. After knocking your opponent's sword down, immediately go for his arms or wrists with your blade.

Defending against Stabbing

The stabbing action can be a scary situation because it presents us with a small visual target as opposed to a bigger line of action. When defending against a stab you need to be sensitive enough to be aware of it. The threat is increased when dealing with a real sword because the tip is even narrower than that of a wooden practice sword. The practice sword has a round tip, but a metal sword has a point that forms a very narrow line when viewed head-on!

Counter Strike as You Escape forward

The typical and wise choice is to step off the centerline as the stab is headed straight for you. It would be a good choice to use the circling escape step off the centerline. This is the same principle you would use for a straight punch or kick, for that matter. The straight-line attack, like the stab, is very weak against the circle line, which is more diverse.

Figure 7.20

Figure 7.20 shows a side step to the left that puts you in a safe zone and allows you to counterattack from a generally safe range. Figure 7.21 shows a similar principle with more of a diagonal step to the left front side, which is safer for you as well as more aggressive to your opponent who is coming into your range. As the attack comes and you step to the side, push your arms and sword downward to block the attack with your blade. If you step more aggressively into a forward stance your counter-attack will be that much more powerful.

Figure 7.21

Countering with a Single Hand Strike

This technique shares some similarities with the previous one. You are sidestepping to the left while deflecting the attack with your sword held in your left hand only.

Figure 7.22

This puts you into a safer position in a range farther from your opponent, while allowing you to conservatively extend only your arm toward the attack. After deflecting the attack you would stab to the chest or throat area of your opponent. While the single hand counter keeps you farther away from your opponent, using only one hand on the sword is weaker and gives you less control of your sword and less power to penetrate the target with your counterattack.

Redirecting the Stab in the Seigan Position, then Returning

The general principle of this technique is to keep your movements to a minimum. Stay in the *Seigan* position, keeping your sword in contact with your opponent's sword. As you feel pressure from your opponent's movement, redirect their sword to the outside of your body range to make them miss you. Don't parry their sword with too much force because you need to return for a counterattack quickly and you don't want to give them a second chance to make another action. It will take practice to cultivate a subdued parry.

In Figure 7.23 you can see that you need to keep a good amount of space between your body and the sword to avoid a strike. If you don't have enough space your opponent's tip will reach you before you parry it.

Figure 7.23

Figure 7.24

As shown in Figure 7.24, you need to deftly turn your sword into a stabbing position. At this moment, your blade is turned to the left (toward your opponent's sword) in case they try to attack again. This is safer than if your blade is at a more vertical angle. Figure 7.25 shows the front view of your position. Figure 7.26 shows how the preceding two techniques are actually happening in one quick step instead of in two steps. This means you are executing both the defensive and offensive techniques simultaneously.

In this compound technique, you're skipping the first *Seigan* block. You need to use a little body movement in which you lean your body to the left as you parry by putting your sword into a horizontal angle (as seen in Figure 7.25) at same time. Also, you're using a lower stance so that you're prepared for an immediate counter. The blade needs to face toward the left again. This flat angle of the sword is leading the opponent's sword to the outside of your body. As you keep your sword in contact with your opponent's sword you will be in the process of countering with a stab as well. Figures 7.23 and 7.24 show the process of blocking and countering. Figure 7.26 shows immediate countering occurring simultaneously with the blocking maneuver.

Figure 7.25

Figure 7.26

Flicking the Opponent's Sword away from Your Body with an Inward Block

This technique is very similar to the application of the last part of the basic *kata*. This single-handed downward block is a very weak block by itself, so you have to position your body at an angle to avoid your opponent's sword. Make sure you're

Figure 7.27

Figure 7.28

Figure 7.29

Figure 7.30

protecting yourself by turning your body to present a narrower profile. So in other words, you're primarily avoiding the blow by moving your body; the hand block is just insurance for your safety.

In order to execute this technique, please review the explanation of the arm and hand movement found in step 9 of Chapter 6, *Kata Practice*. You are essentially inviting your opponent into your range by using your arm in a circle block in order to put your opponent's body in front of you to take a counter without your having to make so many extra steps. To turn your block into a counterattack you would swing your sword around overhead after receiving the stab and use the rebound to do this. Your holding position will be the *Kesa* position for a very short moment to turn it into a diagonal strike back toward your opponent. Your whole body action is making a parry rather than crashing against the attack.

The following analogy may help you to envision this technique. Imagine you are a tornado and your opponent is on a path to intercept. As soon as he touches the tornado, he begins to turn with it.

The Three Count Drill

Once your opponent receives your first strike, you have the choice of making an escaping step to neutralize the moment or staying engaged in that moment to receive their return.

The third count is an escaping step. Make sure your escape spot is relatively inconvenient for your opponent's pursuit. For instance, a bad example would be

Figure 7.31

to back up in a straight line. Use your wits and creativity to practice by using any combination you can spontaneously execute from memory in order to make an escaping step away from the situation.

The most important element of this escape is for you to find the spot that is the most awkward for your opponent and most convenient for yourself. This is the common thread in any counter-action.

Refer to Figure 7.31. In this case, you have escaped to your opponent's weak spot. Her body position and stance are opened toward you, but you are balanced and you can turn into an aggressive stance faster than she is able to make another step to reach you.

You are making sure that the tip of the sword is pointed toward your opponent, and your opponent's sword is pointed toward you as well. In fact, it's important for your opponent to keep her sword pointed toward you. Her defensive position requires her to maintain a threatening posture if she is to continue the engagement.

The Wrist Counter

The Wrist Counter is good for saving time. You are countering on an offbeat or rhythm, so the opponent will be in an awkward position. Your sword is reaching *them*, not their sword. And if you are in a situation facing multiple opponents, this choice is going to be even more helpful.

This is a quick interception of your opponent's attack and it will put them in an awkward position as you take them by surprise. You should strive to catch your opponent in the transition from starting their attack (inhaling) and before they get their full strength into the attack (exhaling).

This counter technique doesn't require any significant power on your part—it's all about timing and distance.

The occasion to use this technique is when your opponent is over-extending in an attempt to reach you. If you can hit your opponent's sword in that moment when they are in this weaker position (not rooted in a neutral stance) you can do the job without much exertion.

Figure 7.32

Offense by Invitation

In these techniques, you will purposefully "show" a vulnerable spot to draw the first action from your opponent. This can be very dangerous for you.

Waiting and Inviting with Your Sword in the Downward Position

In this technique, you will strike their sword very powerfully from below.

You begin by appearing to be in a careless position, but in this downward position you are actually quite ready to spring into action. As you can see from the slight elevation of the sword, it's not really pointing straight down to the ground; the outward edge is angled toward your opponent. In Figure 7.34, you can see that the upraised sword is ready to receive the strike at the beginning of the stroke. This will

Figure 7.33

check her sword force early in the strike rather than waiting to receive it later in the attack. As you might expect, that would be too late because her sword is about to cut you on the shoulder line. The tip of your sword should dip toward your opponent to lend strength to your block. Refer to Figure 7.34 for a side view of this blocking

Figure 7.34

action. Finally, as shown in Figure 7.35, you simply take a big step forward to reach your opponent immediately after flicking her sword away. As you step in, your *tsuka/* sword hilt should be pushed towards your opponent's hilt to restrict another attack. This technique boasts simple footwork similar to that of fencing, and the sword action is more reminiscent of sliding then swinging.

Figure 7.35

Waiting and Inviting as you Hold Your Sword in a Side Waki Gamae Chambered Position

In this variation, you are holding sword right against your hip bone. You will escape to a safe zone to the left as you are receiving your opponent's sword with a roof block. Then swing your sword all the way around from behind your back over your head in order to strike down on your opponent's arm or shoulder.

Figure 7.36

You have to be able to read your opponent's breathing to anticipate their actions. If you only pay attention to their physical movements you're likely to miss subtle cues that could make the difference between life and death. You use the roof block (see Figure 7.37) to make sure you can safely escape to a more defensible position. It's just like running in the rain with your umbrella up. The degree of receiving strength needs to be equivalent to a parry. If you can successfully slide her blade down your own without giving much resistance to your opponent, it may cause her to be thrown off balance as in Figure 7.38, making it easier for you to counter.

As you can see in Figures 7.37 and 7.38, your back foot needs to step forward in order to be able to make your final strike. If, instead of stumbling forward, your opponent gets repelled backwards (as in Figure 7.39), you will still be able to follow through with the same action—your point of contact will be the only difference.

Figure 7.37

Figure 7.38

Figure 7.39

If circumstances permit, you may be able to grab your opponent's shoulder or sleeve with your left hand in order to steady her for your follow-through action. If this opportunity becomes available you may even have the luxury of being able to slightly reposition your opponent to give your strike maximum effectiveness.

Pretending to Relax but Remaining Ready to Strike

Keep your blade out an inward position prepared for immediate action. Go with the flow in the each moment.

When you walk around with your sword you are in regular stance, but you still need to be able to react spontaneously and quickly. This relaxed stance is the antithesis of someone who is holding a sword in a threatening manner (like baseball bat). Your sword is just hanging down from your hand and the tip is not pointed directly at your opponent.

Figure 7.40

You will notice in Figure 7.40 that the sword tip doesn't dip too low and the blade is actually kept somewhat more horizontal than vertical. The blade is also angled slightly away from you, which will help to prevent accidental injury.

CHAPTER 8

SURVIVAL
TECHNIQUES

*Birth and death are always with us, so focus
on being luminous by understanding life.*

There may be times when you find that you're forced to defend yourself from a position of weakness. Perhaps your opponent has a longer-range weapon, or you are attacked while sitting or kneeling. Perhaps you are ambushed while not wearing a sword, or you've been disarmed. Perhaps you've been forced to surrender, and now suspect you are about to be executed. These are life threatening, do-or-die situations, but take heart: with luck and good timing, you can survive them—if you're prepared.

Defending with a Dagger

If you don't carry a weapon equal to your opponent but surrender is not an option, use a *wakizashi/shyoutou* (dagger).

Unless you are fortunate enough to be using a dagger to deal with an attack in close quarters, you'll quickly find that practically every aspect of the situation begs for a longer weapon with greater range and power. On the other hand, the benefits of using a dagger lie in its compact size and quick deployment.

It goes without saying that if you are defending yourself against a sword attack with a dagger you are obviously at a significant disadvantage because of the limited range of your weapon. Use this tactic only as a last resort!

Defense against a Vertical Strike

Against a vertical strike, step and turn your body diagonally. Grab part of your opponent's arm to restrict a second action, and then put your blade to their throat.

It's very important that you elicit an ill-advised and unsuccessful strike from your opponent. It doesn't mean that you need to commence a series of risky footwork maneuvers to entice a strike. If you allow your focus to waver you might make a critical mistake.

Stay calm and focused, but keep your mind alert enough to be ready for the moment of action.

As your opponent strikes, step out of her striking line and step forward at a 45-degree angle. Take another step towards your opponent and raise your empty hand to restrain your opponent's closest arm. It's fine to grab with an underhanded grip, but be careful to turn your palm at the last moment so that you don't expose critical veins that run along the inside of your arm.

Figure 8.1

Figure 8.2

After you secure your opponent's arm, put your blade to her throat without any hesitation. Make sure you hold your opponent's arm securely throughout this action.

If you are successful in dodging the original attack move in immediately to press your attack and don't let go—you aren't likely to get another shot at this. And this is so important: you need to apply significant pressure against your opponent's neck in order to convince them to surrender.

Figure 8.3

Defending against a Diagonal Arcing Slash

Against a diagonal arcing slash, duck beneath and let it pass by. In the next instant grab your opponent's elbow, and strike or stab the body area that is most available to your weapon hand.

Figure 8.4

Figure 8.5

This is very similar to first technique. Let your opponent follow through with her choice of action and then take control by stepping into her blind spot with a grab and a thrust of your blade to the side of her body to let her know its a done deal. But if you miss your mark or are too stingy with the pressure behind the blade, your adversary may not adequately fear the danger and may opt to attempt escape rather than surrender.

Figure 8.6

Defending against a Horizontal Cut

Against a horizontal cut, wrap your left arm around your opponent's arms as you step in to close the distance and press the blade to their throat.

Figure 8.7

To do this you need to grasp the dagger in the point down configuration as shown in Figures 8.7 through 8.9. Your opponent will try to reach you with her sword in a horizontal stroke. After you dodge the stroke and you need to quickly step into the area on side of her body where the horizontal cut originated.

As you're stepping ahead diagonally, raise your left arm high to accommodate your opponent's arms (see Figure 8.8, where I've exaggerated the motion a bit for the purposes of this demonstration). When you execute this move, don't just raise your arm—make sure you step deeply (at a 45-degree angle) toward your opponent's arms. You need to do this to securely arrest your opponent's ability to swing the sword. This restriction will only occur when you successfully tuck both of your opponent's wrists/elbows under your armpit. This effectively wraps your opponent's

Figure 8.8

wrists/elbows wrists and squeezes them tight. If done properly, your opponent's elbows and wrists will be locked, and she'll have lost control over her sword. The restricted blade should remain safely immobilized in a line parallel to your forearm.

Figure 8.9

Using Double Swords against a Staff

A caveat: using two swords might look good in the movies but, in reality, it tends to hobble you by tying up both of your hands with less-than-optimal single-handed grips on the swords. Samurai swords were designed for double-handed use, which makes the sword's application very efficient and effective. Even when simply swinging the sword around, a double-handed grip will allow you to be faster than you would if using only a single-handed grip. On the other hand, the beauty of using a double sword technique is that you can come up with a greater variety of attacks and blocks.

The staff can be a very formidable weapon in the hands of someone who knows how to use it well, however, its application is fairly straightforward. So, with two swords, you'll use a more complex technique to deal with a simple one. For that reason, you must be adept with using this technique in order to pull it off successfully.

You cannot allow your opponent remain at their preferred distance with a longer-range weapon like a staff. You need to manipulate the situation so that it favors the range of your weapons, not theirs.

In this technique, you'll be using double swords to create an X block, but the block needs to be executed at a diagonal angle toward your opponent rather than exactly straight up. If you block vertically you'll give them the chance to swing the other

Figure 8.10

Figure 8.11

Figure 8.12

Figure 8.13

Figure 8.14

end of the staff around for a second strike. Another thing to note is that the double swords maneuver is not a very convenient choice if you need to be quick.

As shown in Figure 8.10, your swords should remain in a downward position to invite the high-level staff attack. As shown in Figure 8.11, you'll receive the attack with a high block with the blades pointed outward as you cross both swords over each other. This is sometimes called a "scissors block" for obvious reasons. This high block will stop the downward stroke of your opponent's staff.

This will result in an awkward position for your opponent because, at this point, it's not to her advantage to pull back *or* push forward. Your opponent might opt to bring about the other end of the staff to try to hit you, but at this point you have the advantage with solid contact with the staff. If necessary, you can simply slide your swords down the staff with the aim of cutting your opponent's hands, as seen in Figure 8.12.

At this point your opponent will likely decide to disengage from your swords and withdraw to regroup (Figure 8.13). Step in immediately and chase her hands without giving her a chance to retreat (Figure 8.14).

Keep in mind; if you allow your opponent to retreat, she'll have another opportunity to use her weapon's long distance advantage against you to possibly disastrous effect. It's best to end the confrontation while you maintain the advantageous distance.

Sword Techniques from a Kneeling Position

Traditionally, when sitting, keeping your sword on your left side means "alert" and the right side means "disarmed" for courtesy.

Usually, *Battou* means that you are just drawing your sword out of its scabbard. But it's also possible to turn *Battou* into an offensive strike at the same time while in either the standing or sitting position.

Battou: Drawing Your Sword for an Offensive Action

Make sure that your partner sits still and you don't go too fast. Pay attention to your technique rather than speed in the beginning. You are using your partner for aim, but your partner is not there just to be your target like a wooden dummy. All martial arts practice is like a conversation. The receiving partner should also be involved and get some exercise or benefit out of the practice. In this instance your partner

Figure 8.15

is training his own powers of perception. In this situation, he needs to be a good listener and think about how to receive an offensive action. If you want to improve your speed once you get the technique down, do it later without a partner for safety.

Cutting through: Turning Your Scabbard Horizontally

Use your thumb to flip your scabbard sideways so that the sword blade faces outward from your body to make the sword flat (parallel to the floor) so it's ready to draw out in a horizontal line. In this way, the blade is already facing toward the object in front of you. Keep the *kissaki*/tip of your blade curved or pointed to the left side as you make your cut so that you make your cut with the blade and don't throw the *kissaki* at the target. In order to do this you need to keep your knuckles up. Cut through your target on a horizontal plane.

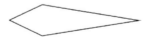

The diagram shows the blade position in relation to your body (left of the diagram).

Figure 8.16

Cutting up: Do Not Turn Your Scabbard

The sword will make the cutting line of a reversed *Kesa*/diagonal up toward sky. Keep your blade down as you pull it out of the scabbard, and then turn it as you extend your arm overhead. Imagine, a bird opening its wings gracefully.

Figure 8.17

Cutting down: Turn Your Wrist up (Blade up)

Your thumb sits on the blade side of the scabbard (curved side) and turns it toward the sky like in Figure 8.15. Draw out the sword as you turn your body partially toward the sword to compensate for the tight space that you have in which to draw it out. In the first moment of drawing the sword, it's almost as if you're tossing the sword hilt toward the target, but then flip the sword to make the blade reach out. The stroke will resolve into a straight vertical line from head to floor.

Figure 8.18

Countering by Swinging Your Scabbard into the inside of Your Opponent's Knee

This is an off-balancing way of dealing with an attack without drawing your sword out. As your opponent begins to draw out their sword, swing your sheathed sword with your right hand on the hilt and left hand on the scabbard into your opponent's knee to off set him off balance. Immediately afterwards, you should to prepare to draw your sword and ready yourself for a second strike. With your scabbard still in front of you, push the tip of the scabbard into your opponent's stomach. The scabbard's tip will immediately go under his right arm. Don't bring the tip over his right arm unless he is already in a lower position because it's generally too far of a reach for the tip to go over his arm. Don't waste your time trying to reach over your opponent's arm unless the situation warrants it. Also, as long as your left hand is low, you can raise it to restrict your opponent's right hand—just in case he continues to draw his sword.

If, for whatever reason, your opponent recovers without getting knocked off balance by your initial strike, you should consider drawing your sword as your are striking at his stomach with the scabbard and also using it to restrict the movement of his forward arm. It's a more natural choice to push straight towards your opponent using your left hand by using the vertical fist you've already formed to grasp your scabbard.

Figure 8.19

Figure 8.20

Using the Scabbard to Restrict the Opponent's Drawing Hand and Striking His Throat

As you see in the Figure 8.21, you are in a lower position than your opponent. Though conventional thought is that you are at a disadvantage, you will use that position to your technical advantage. Drag your scabbard across your opponent's right arm and keep it there to put solid pressure on the arm to inhibit his drawing action. Then strike his throat at a diagonal upward angle. It's preferable not to grasp your scabbard by wrapping your left thumb to the opposite side as your fingers because this will restrict your movements to a certain degree. And besides, you don't need the additional power that a fully formed left fist would afford because you are using your opponent's arm as a stable pivoting point. Instead, grab the scabbard with four fingers to keep your left hand free (see Figure 8.21), so if something goes wrong, you can use it for another grab.

Draw your sword while you are simultaneously striking your opponent's throat with the end of your scabbard. Bring the sword around your back shoulder with a big circular motion for a smooth draw. This will also make sure that you don't cut your own forearm, which could easily happen if you fail to follow the circular path. Slide the scabbard along your opponent's right arm with a liberal amount of pressure as you draw your sword. At the end of this maneuver, your scabbard is restricting both your opponent's wrist and *tsuka*/hilt.

Figure 8.21

Figure 8.22

Figure 8.23

Figure 8.24

Avoiding Sword Action and Going into Jyu-jitsu Action Immediately

You always have the choice to react without a sword. Keep your left hand palm down to trap your opponent's front arm while your right hand is grabbing his neck/shoulder (if he's wearing heavy material, you can grab that instead). Your left hand can either pull your opponent's right arm or push his right elbow inward. Your right

Figure 8.25

Figure 8.26

hand/arm is pushing on the neck or shoulder in order to turn your opponent to your left and take them down. While you're executing the takedown your face should be tucked behind his right shoulder for protection.

Protecting Your Sword from Being Taken and Going into a Counter Action

In this case, for whatever reason, you were delayed in your reaction. Trap both of your opponent's hands right on the hilt by your pushing them forcefully down to the ground. Give your opponent's throat a left elbow strike. Switch your hands, now using your left hand to grab the scabbard near the sword hilt to trap his right

Figure 8.27

hand on the hilt. Use your right hand to pull the scabbard upward with a quick and strong snap to withdraw the scabbard smoothly. Keeping the scabbard partly on the sword, turn the blade side toward your opponent and aim it the exposed blade directly at his throat. Be careful not to pull the scabbard completely off, as you will lose control of the sword. The blade is now right against your opponent's neck artery, which is obviously a very dangerous location.

Figure 8.28

Figure 8.29

Figure 8.30

Figure 8.31

Restricting the Opponent's Drawing Hand with Your Scabbard and Putting the Blade to His Throat

Quickly step up to your opponent's right drawing hand. Keep your right hand on your scabbard and use your left hand to grab his hilt to restrict his ability to draw the sword. Keep your sword up in front to reach your opponent's hand faster. You are almost leaning into his sword in order to trap it. Shift your body weight backwards a little to prepare for drawing your own sword without making any steps. In other words, you are making extra space to draw your sword by doing this. But don't shift back too far because your opponent will still attempt to attack. So draw your sword as soon as you sense that there is enough space between you and your opponent. Continue to restrict his arm as you draw your sword.

Figure 8.32

Figure 8.33

Figure 8.34

Disarming Techniques

It's very dangerous to go against an armed opponent empty-handed, but you will have to if you are in a "do or die" situation. Use the outside of your body as it has thinner veins compared to the arteries found in the inward facing parts of your body. If you get cut on the outer part of your arm, it's not as critical as getting cut on the inside of your arm. Being cut on an artery will disable you more quickly.

The Leg Sweep Disarming Technique

You used the same basic technique in the sitting position discussed earlier in this chapter. Your opposite hand will restrict your opponent's drawing hand immediately and your closer hand will trap his neck or shoulder. This will restrict him from drawing his sword. Then you sweep your opponent's leg as he tries to get out of the trap. Yank your opponent toward you to redirect him. Because he doesn't want to fall with his sword it's likely that he will pull backward to stay upright. Shift tactics and go with your opponent, pushing him backward now, augmenting his own force in that same direction. Step behind your opponent with your right leg and sweep his right leg by hitting

Figure 8.35

Figure 8.36

Figure 8.37

his calf with yours while your hands are pulling and turning his upper body into the ground at same time to take him down.

The Leg Sweep Disarming Technique: Variation A

In this technique you will trap your opponent's arm to restrict him from drawing his sword, and strike his throat at the same time (see Figure 8.38). Then you'll move straight in to knock him backwards (Figure 8.39).

Figure 8.38   **Figure 8.39**

It's almost a non-stop movement in the same straight direction, so you can run into your opponent if you are able to do so. You are essentially running straight through your opponent with this technique. Your right hand traps his forearm firmly with your first step. At the same time use your left fist with the middle finger second knuckle pointed up for a sharper strike to the throat. If this action knocks him backwards, you will follow through as you grab either your opponent's hair or ear as your right hand continues to strongly trap his arm against his body. Use this moment when your opponent is off balance to sweep his leg for a takedown.

The Leg Sweep Disarming Technique: Variation B

Avoid the horizontal strike by using "replace step" (retreating with the left leg and stepping in with the right), letting the sword pass by. Immediately after the sword passes step in close to your opponent, keeping your right arm down so that you may trap both his arms (Figure 8.41). Trap his arms with yours (Figure 8.42) and take a big step back with your right foot as you drop your weight down (Figure 8.43). Use this step and weight shift to yank your opponent's arms toward you by hooking both your

Figure 8.40

Figure 8.41

Figure 8.42

Figure 8.43

Figure 8.44

hands and fingers on his inner elbow joints. His body will begin to fall forward but your opponent won't want to keep falling in that direction, so when he pulls backwards, follow him and sweep his leg with your right leg as your arms are restricting and pushing his arms at the same time.

The Arm Immobilizing Technique

Use your belt or any tough material to trap your opponent's arms. Wrap both his forearms either after his swing or before it (intercept it—see Figures 8.45 through 8.47). After you've wrapped the forearms, squeeze your hands and arms downward toward the ground. Your left foot is initially in behind your opponent's right foot but it will step through in front of his stance as you lift his arms over your left shoulder to carry them up. Now, you and your opponent are facing the same direction (Figure 8.48). He has to deal with pain in his elbows as you squeeze and pull your arms down. Then tilt your left shoulder forward for the take down. His body will follow.

Figure 8.45

Figure 8.46

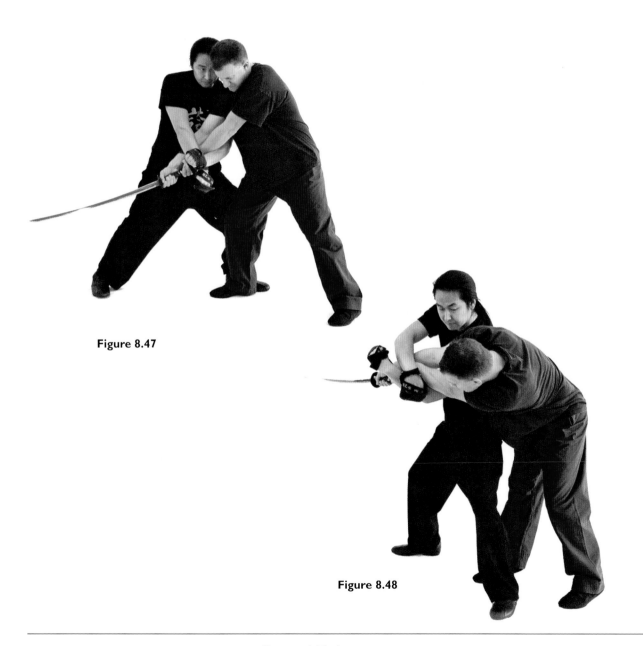

Figure 8.47

Figure 8.48

Figure 8.49

The Blade Trapping Technique

In the technique, you'll escape from a first strike and then grab the backside (dull, non-bladed side) of your opponent's sword.

Let the blade pass (Figure 8.50) then trap the end of the hilt immediately with your left hand by grabbing your opponent's hand or wrist. If your hand is smaller than his, don't worry about grabbing the whole area; just grab near the end of the hand around the pinky muscle group. But hook your finger into it like a hawk claw. Your right hand grabs the backside of the blade with your right hand by pinching it between your thumb and pointer and middle fingers (Figure 8.51). Step

Figure 8.50

forward with your right foot with a big half circle step in front of your opponent. Push your left hand down on his hilt and push your right hand and elbow up to make the blade turn into him. Your right elbow is essentially making a big boxing

Figure 8.51   **Figure 8.52**

hook punch to his chin. This will cause an extreme turning of his grip and disarm him, becoming a counter-offensive at the same time (Figure 8.52).

Close-Range Techniques

Because the *katana/daitou* is a long weapon, it's not a good choice for a close range encounter, but you still have options. Stay close to your opponent and follow his actions. Use your blade and tip without making wide swings; you will have to use pressure, sliding (up or down), and pulling—it's almost like playing a violin.

- You are standing to the outside of your opponent's lead arm and your sword is pressed on his forearm. Maintain this pressure between your arm and his to be able to slide your sword smoothly. It's very important to keep your left arm stable and be sure to keep the outside of your forearm turned toward your opponent to keep your artery away from the sword in case you

Figure 8.53

get cut. You should be putting pressure on your opponent's sword at a diagonal angle downward rather than straight down. You may notice that if you push the hilt with your right hand, it will turn into a stabbing action.

Figure 8.54

- This is the same principle as the first choice but you are in a forward stance (aggressively step in with your front knee bent). This stabbing can be alternatively aimed at their stomach as well. Aim the tip of your sword toward your opponent's throat with your blade pressing near his elbow joint. Your forearm pressures his right biceps and the pinky side of your fist is pressuring on the sword (instead of using your wrist). You should be able to retreat backwards or to the side even though you are in wide stance.

- Your blade is turned up toward your opponent and you are pressing your sword down onto your opponent's sword. Use your forearm to pressure the *mune*/non-bladed side of your opponent's sword. Your sword is cutting upward toward the outside of his forearm.

Figure 8.55

- Use your regular grip but with a sawing action.

Figure 8.56

- This is a sort of a high or roof block. Your left elbow supports the backside of the sword. In Figure 8.57, it looks like your elbow is in peril but it's actually protected by the combination of the forearm restriction on his right wrist and your blade is stopping the root of his blade as it has been sandwiched. You are in a forward stance that means you are stopping his attack before his swinging action reaches full potency. And if you can receive the attack with your blade on his fingers is even better. In that way, you can combine offensive and defensive techniques in one quick maneuver. In this case you lift your left forearm up, flipping his sword over, and make a large circular motion with your sword. You bring the sword to his left ear by bringing your right elbow back down to your hip. Your sword will be directly on his and he will be defenseless.

Figure 8.57

- This is an action of interception. Take a big step up to your right into his range before his swing reaches its full speed. Your left hand is restraining the end of his hilt by holding your hand in a reversed upward angle to push outward and to the left. It's okay to have your left armpit open by lifting your arm. Move your blade to his ribcage at the same time. Both your right hand and left hand actions should be happening simultaneously.

Figure 8.58

NOTE: The first four techniques in Figures 8.53, 8.54, and 8.55 can be a nice combination or flow as one technique. The other two techniques in Figures 8.57 and 8.58 can be another flow.

Combination one would be as follows: In Figure 8.53 you are stopping the attack. In Figure 8.54 you slice with a big step in. In Figure 8.55 you flip the sword around his forearm to go under it. And finally in Figure 8.56 you switch step from left to right to swing the sword around over your head for a Kesa cut.

Techniques against an Opponent with the Advantage

You are in a lower position and your opponent is standing, possibly with his sword in hand. In this technique you'll strongly draw your sword out to make first contact and knock his sword away from your range. You will use a different type of drawing in this case. The tip will go out first and you'll pull your hilt back to your side immediately, so the sword will create a strong snapping effect to his sword in order to flick it away. As soon as your sword re-directs his to the ground you attack his legs instead of standing up. This attack from your lower position is going to be quicker for you to execute and will take place at an awkward angle for him to defend.

Figure 8.59

Figure 8.60

In Figure 8.59, you are carefully watching his shoulder and arm for the right timing as you prepare to draw your sword. Don't pay too much attention to the sword or it will be too late for you to react. The sword could disappear from your view since it can make a very thin line in the air. You should watch his shoulder and hand, and listen to his breathing.

In Figure 8.60, you are knocking the backside of his sword to redirect it and you are also ducking under his sword at the same time. Aim for his wrist for the contact point—it's more sure than aiming for his blade. Flick the sword tip outward by turning your wrist upward quickly and retracting your elbow toward your body a little.

Figure 8.61

In Figure 8.61, you are keeping his sword touching the ground by letting your sword lay on top of his. Start to move around to his blind spot behind his right leg.

In Figure 8.62, you're you cutting your opponent's right leg while moving into his blind spot.

And in Figure 8.63, you have successfully made it behind him and cut his leg at same time. While you're moving behind your opponent, it's crucial that you move smoothly and stay in the kneeling position. You need to practice this without a sword in your hand to be able to walk on the ground without standing up.

Figure 8.62

Figure 8.63

. . . .

You've reached the end of the sword technique instruction. If you practice and master these techniques, your skills will serve you well in a conflict. It will be even more beneficial if your mastery allows you to avoid the fight altogether. As good as these techniques are, it's not enough to rely on physical techniques alone. Proceed to the next chapter, "Mental Conditioning," to find out why.

CHAPTER 9

MENTAL
CONDITIONING

黙想

*If the hawk is educated, he does not show
his claw unless he needs to.*

*We are all born with points of light within,
we just need to keep up a healthy conversation
with them. Yes, you are a piece of God.*

Ultimately, the goal of practicing martial arts is not just about developing good physical techniques. More importantly, the purpose of practicing martial arts is to develop one's inner self. Physically you desire to be healthy and be able to defend your family and yourself. And internally you want to be strong as well by growing mentally, emotionally, and spiritually. After all, to physically hurt someone should be the last resort in a self-defense situation. If you are strong on the inside hopefully you will have the ability to defuse a confrontation with no one getting hurt.

Also, it's very important that what you learn in the martial arts translates into the other areas of your life. Perseverance, spirit, control and respect are just a few of the terms that are regularly spoken about in the dojo (martial arts school). These qualities are not just used during a fight. They are used in every day life experiences. And in order to utilize these qualities in the best possible manner you must keep yourself focused in an increasingly demanding environment. Meditation is a great tool that you can use to keep yourself focused. Two types of meditation you will examine are *mokusou* and *meisou*.

Mokusou means silent or quiet thought. Why do you need to do this? It's good to neutralize (clean up) the distracting "noisy" thoughts from your mind. Your thoughts are "vibrations" made by your brain. The brain makes these vibrations constantly—even when you are sleeping. Left unchecked these vibrations can get out of control. If you stay in this negative stage of vibration too long, it tends to cause stress that may lead to physical problems such as illness or disease. Though your physical condition is influenced by outside forces, sometimes the brain can influence your condition leading to illness as well. You need to be careful of this. Your brain is the main computer that controls your whole body. It gives orders to every part of the body, but that doesn't mean the brain is thinking about everything. Sometimes your body parts need to send signals to the brain.

A respectable and honorable sword will stay in its scabbard;

And so will human beings.

For example, your body's organs work involuntarily. Your heart pumps blood through the body and your stomach digests the food you eat. You don't have to think about how these organs function. They just do what they do. But if they start to act up, a signal is sent to the brain to let you know that you need to take a look at

what's going on inside. Even when you aren't receiving signals from your body, you take time to see your doctor for regular physical exams so that they can check out your organs to make sure they are working properly.

I am one with the universe.

As for your brain and your mental, emotional, and spiritual states, if you cannot find the answers in your life, then that may lead to a headache whether literally or figuratively. Hopefully you can use *mokusou* to catch any of these problems before they lead to that headache. In other words, you can call *mokusou* a time of reflection. The purpose of this reflection is to commune with yourself. It gives you a chance to review your daily thoughts and actions so that you may find the right answers in your life. If you don't take the time to look inside yourself, it's not easy to find those answers. *Mokusou* gives you the opportunity to step out of your regular routine or pattern in order to discover what is working for you and discard what is not working.

神道 **Shinto** is "The Way of God." It's an ancient Japanese philosophy of teaching and faith. The Native Americans also follow this living principle.

The way of the samurai is strongly rooted in Shinto and Zen Buddhism. That is why it's very important to connect to nature (Shinto teaches to accept environmental messages) and recognize feelings (Zen teaches to find your internal truth). You should train to be able to feel or recognize all the vibrations or spirit within

A Shinto shrine is designed to house Kami—the spirits of the Shinto faith.

everything. In this way, we can say God *is everywhere*. Practicing *mokousou* and *meisou* will help you to realize these principles within you.

The bridge between meditation and Shinto is *satori*. *Satori* means to notice, awaken, and realize. Many people say that martial arts practice is a way of life. *Satori* talks about life. As humans we go through many events with the purpose of growing our souls. In Shinto, *satori* applies to the relationship between humans and God, and closing the difference between the two. The relationship between *satori* and meditation is that *satori* tells us that it's much easier to change or control ourselves than it is to change others. The best way to change others is to change ourselves and lead by example. If we introduce a good example to others, they will learn from our example, and this can be contagious.

The purpose of *mokusou* is to re-condition the brain to keep good "vibrations" and let you do what you need to do without having chaos in your mind.

Shimenawa

In martial arts practice this applies to the concept of combat as well. The whole condition of combat is a contradiction. This is because in one way combat asks you to stay calm and in control while on the other hand you need to be alert and aggressive. We see the same thing in our everyday routines. Though we are always seeking happiness, in order to achieve it we are constantly working.

And we call them a "Peaceful Warrior/Peace Maker."

God will increase his power by man's respect. A man will gain fortune by God's virtue.

In martial arts practice, it's very important to have *mokusou* time before and after practice. Before training the purpose of *mokusou* is to clear your mind from your regular life routine in order to release your extra tension. This also prepares you to focus and accept everything you will learn during your lesson.

Mokusou time after training will bring calmness to your heart as you re-enter your regular life routine without holding onto the anxiety from practice.

A deeper form of meditation is *meisou*. *Meisou* is performed with sunlight or candlelight. *Meisou* may be done facing the sun or not as you keep your eyes half opened, (called *hangan*). This allows you to take the sunlight into you. This practice will result in effective cleansing of your body and spirit as sunlight is the life force. If sunlight is not available, candlelight may be used in its place. The candle's flame vibration has a deep and positive effect on the mind. The use of the candle during meditation has been happening all over the world throughout history.

The performance of *meisou* should take place during daylight hours. The best time to perform *meisou* is during the morning while the sun is rising. If performed after sundown, *meisou* is spiritually unsafe. It is especially unsafe to do *meisou* between 12 AM and 4 AM. During these hours we are supposed to be at rest.

When someone becomes good at these practices, they will notice positive results in breathing, sleep and more. This rejuvenation will especially show more shine in your eyes.

When you sweep the dust out of your mind and spirit, the light can shine again.

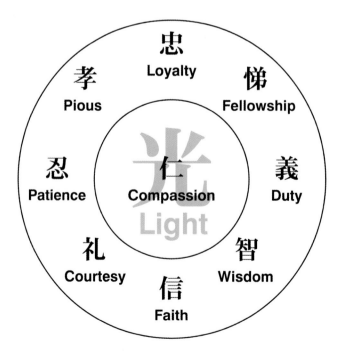

Harmony is virtuous. Let it flow smoothly.

This is a great essence of the martial arts journey and practice. It includes the 陰 **In** and 陽 **Yo** (Yin and Yang) principle of balance. While most people focus on the physical practice, it's just as important to take care of the internal as this internal space is the bigger and more serious space.

Let's start actual practice

First, sit down on a floor that is not concrete or too hard or cold. You should make sure you feel comfortable sitting on the floor. Make sure you are in a good position of either 正座 **Seiza** (formal sitting position) where your legs are bent with your feet under you (above left). Or sit with your legs crossed in front of you (above right). Keep your upper body very straight without any tension. Keep your back straight from the tailbone to the top of your head.

Ask yourself step-by-step to relax your:

• Knees	• Chest	• Elbows	• Neck	• Temple
• Stomach	• Arms	• Shoulders	• Jaw	• Forehead

Once you have the proper sitting position with your body in a relaxed place, you must concentrate on breathing properly. You need to breathe deeply into your lungs so that oxygen goes through your entire body and into your cells. Shallow tense breaths will not provide clear blood circulation and will not circulate the oxygen

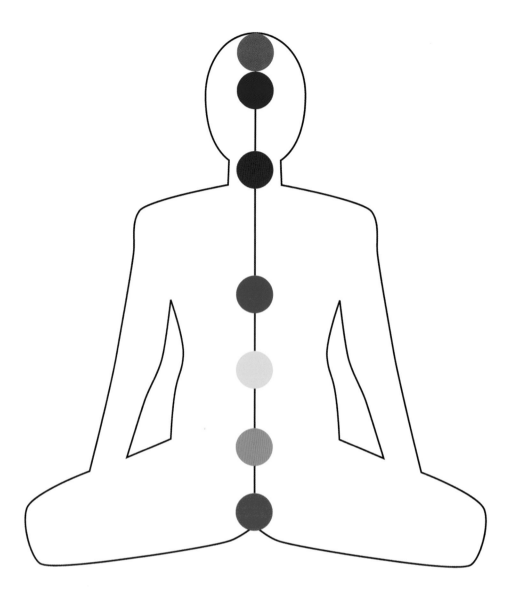

through the body properly. This will leave toxins in your body and will lead you to negatives in physique and thought. A parallel can be drawn to the food you eat. Good, or non-toxic, foods will help you both physically and emotionally. While poor food choices will make you ill or overweight.

This diagram shows where the main chakras are in the body. The corresponding chart on the opposite page describes the significance of each point.

As you breathe deeply, feel the positive energy flow within your body as if you are being cleansed by a sea breeze. Just feel it for a short while. Then gradually start to listen to your breathing as you hold onto this ideal feeling and attitude. In *mokusou* or *meisou* time, you will create your utopia in your internal world by feeling as well as thinking. Some of us say, "empty your mind" or "do not think anything." But that is not realistic in the beginning stages of practice. Instead, it's better to start with positive feelings and reach the "empty your mind" stage very gradually. It's best to shed stressful feelings by creating an escape zone within you. Stick with it—this is a process. It's better to think "I will have better health in time" rather than telling yourself, "I am in perfect health," even though you are not yet in perfect health. So too will reachable goals encourage you, unlike the false statements that we sometimes use to try to deceive ourselves. Understand that it's okay to have negative thoughts during your meditation time. It is normal to have these thoughts, so accept them. Accepting issues or problems is okay, as you will develop the positive energy to face those issues and the courage to overcome them. Continue to do this and one day soon you will notice that your mental resistance is less than in the beginning and you will be getting closer to the empty mind.

The purpose here is to give a basic idea of what *meisou* practice is all about and how to do it. Ultimately to improve, you should seek a good instructor for your benefit and safety. *Meisou* is not just for reflection. The goal is to develop the seven *chakras* of the body as well. As you might know from yoga exercise, there is physical exercise as well as mind exercises. It is important that you understand and respect how the *chakras* work and what they mean. *Chakras* are life energy spots (light spots). They are connections between our physical body and spiritual body. I recommend that you always take care of them for better living.

Here is basic information about the seven *chakras*:

Terminology	Place	Color	Purpose
1. Mooladhara	Lower private part	Red	Life Force
2. Swadhisthana	Private parts	Orange	Delight
3. Manipura	Solar Plexus	Yellow	Fulfillment
4. Anahata	Chest	Green	Love
5. Vishuddhi	Throat	Blue	Will
6. Ajna	Forehead	Purple	Inspiration
7. Sahasrara	Vertex	White, Gold	Universe

Nature's beauty is always smiling upon us. Out of thankfulness we will take care of the earth.

Mokusou and *meisou* are very similar exercises and they will be beneficial to your life. Once you get into the habit of using this internal practice you will start to regard negative emotions as the foolish feelings that they are. If someone is constantly carrying anger or anxiety in their life, you will also notice that that person is lacking this practice in their life. You might be able to let them know what they are missing in life by your presence and example. If that's the case, then you already have already employed the technique called "winning without a fight." If you can win without a fight you are a respectable, peaceful warrior and wise person. People will appreciate your existence. This means your 士風 **Shi Fuu** (the wind of the samurai) is beginning to reach a high level.

One can probably define *mokusou* as more "reorganizing" and *meisou* as more "purifying." Ancient wise men found that these *chakras* can be a barometer to diagnose integral mental and physical health concerns. If a certain spot of *chakra* energy is not flowing properly, one can guess what is causing the problem and then be better informed in finding the proper way to approach the issue.

In order to do that, you need to be aware of the nature of each chakra. The key is your conscience. You must focus your conscience into the right intention. And once you get used to doing the proper meditation, you can create a good balance between the body and mind. In doing this you can better enjoy martial arts practice as well as life in general. This is called harmony.

As we understand life is a series of contradictions, it's difficult to judge right or wrong sometimes. Because of this we can lose the balance or harmony in our life. So for the martial artist, meditation is extremely important to maintain the balance.

Beautiful things are endowed with strength, and it teaches us to be at harmony with nature.

IRON BODY, ANGEL HEART

Your undertaking will keep your outlook positive. Duty is a magnificent blessing because it is the sign of trust from the universe.

Honor with your heart,
and aim for glory with
Ambition & Persistance

Dear Reader

Thank you for reading my book. It means a lot to me that you took the time to do so. I hope that you enjoyed this brief journey. Though we have never met and maybe never will, at least we have been able to share a few moments through this book. That is very special in itself, and I hope you learned something from this experience.

Once again, the purpose of martial arts is not only about hurting others physically—it's more about using a system to realize your life has a deeper and wider meaning so that you will not miss the beautiful moments and glory of life. In the journey of martial arts the process of evolution challenges true practitioners. You can always be better. There is always more room for improvement. Similarly, if a tree stops growing, it will die. Martial arts practice helps us to realize the true purpose of our life. Combat is not the ultimate reason why we undertake this journey.

I feel a strong sense of honor and a desire to share these important truths of life by illuminating some of my county's culture and legacy for you. Past wars are part of humanity's struggle through history and martial arts history is part of that. That is why it's very important to study the martial arts as a topic for educational scrutiny.

Techniques and skills are important, but they are not everything. We should want to become true warriors who can stand up on our own two feet and act on our own truths. I would like for us to all work together toward the goal of releasing the world from negative conditions. We are going through one of the toughest times in history now, but there always remains a "Light" within us. Remember that the earth is about duality. There are positives and negatives in the world. We need to stand for the positive in order to get rid of as much of the negative as possible. We are seeking the definition of "Justice" beyond ideology, and that lies within the human heart.

I wish for us to stop fighting each other under any name of God. Please be alert and think for yourself. When we fight each other there tends to be a third party who is profiting from our chaos. We are all part of the same family because we are all a piece of God. There is no God that asks its children to kill each other. God gave all of us ultimate power, and that is our consciousness. Each one of us is responsible to re-condition this world. We are capable of changing anything that is in our conscience.

It is my sincere hope that we all awaken to this truth now.

—Kohshyu Yoshida

About the Author

吉田光舟 **Kohshyu Yoshida**

Photo by Hiroki Uno

KOHSHYU YOSHIDA was born and raised in Chiba, Japan. That period in Japan was what Kohshyu calls "hero trendy." By hero trendy, he refers to the proliferation of entertainment focused on showing heroes who had a good heart and compassion. He believes that entertainment is a powerful tool that can be used to pass along positive ideas and values. He was greatly influenced by that entertainment trend. The positive attitudes toward the future that the Japanese had at that time were passed along to their children. But now it seems we rarely see those heroes or their values. What he sees in movies and on TV are drugs and killing with no emotional conflict.

At age ten, Kohshyu decided to be an action hero in films—a positive role model to inspire others. Since then he has focused on training himself in sports and martial arts. At age fourteen, he took a test to enter Japan's top action movie star school and was accepted as the youngest of one hundred students. He has worked in the entertainment industry in Japan and the United States.

Kohshyu has always dedicated himself to his goal of inspiring and touching other people's lives. That motivation has taken him to a greater level as an entertainer, martial artist, and human being. He starred as the Red Ranger on the popular children's TV show, *Mighty Morphin' Power Rangers*. At the same time he choreographed the very successful *Power Rangers* worldwide live tour that started at Universal Studios in 1994. In addition, he has made many live appearances for the Make-A-Wish Foundation, giving hope and courage to those children who fight to survive disease and other difficulties.

Kohshyu has studied martial arts from all over the world and now teaches martial arts in Los Angeles. As a teacher, his primary goal is to mold his students' hearts—honing their physical abilities is a secondary concern.

Kohshyu's film work includes *Blade*, starring Wesley Snipes. More recently, he appeared in *The Last Samurai*, starring Tom Cruise. The *Last Samurai* was a particularly gratifying experience for him as he is a descendant of samurai warriors, and his family heritage has roots in samurai lineage. His ancestor was 善九郎-篤俊 **Zen Kurou Atsu Toshi** (Heike's Samurai) whose name means Virtue and Ninth Man. AtsuToshi means "a man who has a kind heart and magnificent talent and knowledge to help volunteer action around the world." AtsuToshi was the founder of the family's village, around 800 years ago, and Kohshyu's relatives still live there today. His family-crest, established 900 years ago, shows the hawk-feather protecting the butterfly. The butterfly is the symbol of a royal family. The hawk feather is the symbol of a warrior in Japanese history, and also means "God-crest" in southern Japan. A legendary story from ancient times tells of a samurai lord who dreamed that he received a God-horse and hawk-feather crest from the universe. That is why a shrine used the feather as its symbol.

In addition, Kohshyu's great-great-grandfather, 若治 **Wakaji** (meaning "Youth and Healing") was a remarkable ronin in 19th century Japan, which is the same time period as that in the film "The Last Samurai." Wakaji was famous for inventing a sword hidden inside a walking stick, which he used to protect and save many people's lives.

Kohshyu was named after the historical 19th-century last samurai, Takamori Saigou himself. Takamori was the Japanese hero on whose life the film was based.

In its December 1, 2003, edition, the Los Angeles Times published a feature story on Kohshyu. Other American and Japanese magazines, newspapers, and television programs have also done stories on Kohshyu based on his biography and heritage.

Kohshyu believes that if the samurai heart is re-established in today's world, it will be of benefit to all. If we can become better individuals, that will create a better world. He calls this discipline the 民主主義的 士道 **Democratic Samurai**.

A lack of mental discipline often defeats many people. Kohshyu wishes to share the ancient samurai school of thought to condition himself and others to make stronger minds.

Kohshyu is committed to working in both "Light and Shadow." "Light" represents real life. And "Shadow" represents the illusion that is entertainment. Despite the fantasy elements of entertainment, Kohshyu believes that it can pass along positive messages for our benefit.